JOHN JESSOP: *Goldseeker and Educator*

F. Henry Johnson

JOHN JESSOP: Goldseeker and Educator

Founder of the British Columbia School System

Mitchell Press Limited
Vancouver

Printed in Canada
Manufactured at Vancouver by the Publishers
MITCHELL PRESS LIMITED

To Beth, David, Nancy and Elizabeth

Preface

Who was John Jessop, most readers will ask. In the historians' histories he is a cipher. His name occurs nowhere in any of the present histories of British Columbia, much less of Canada.

He is known only to a small coterie of scholars who are interested in the history of Canadian education. Yet he deserved a better fate than anonymity because he, more than any other, was instrumental in establishing the free, non-sectarian school system of British Columbia and setting it on the course it was to follow. As the first Superintendent of Education for that province he helped design the legislation, administer the system, plan the curriculum, provide schools and teachers for the scattered communities of the province, and by paddle-steamer, canoe and on horseback visited and inspected those early schools. Yet throughout British Columbia today no school perpetuates his name.

To shape the school system of what is today the second largest English-speaking province in Canada is surely a contribution to the social history of the province and of the country which deserves to be recorded. This in itself could be deemed sufficient excuse for writing Jessop's biography.

But there is another compelling reason — the fact that the man is so little known, that he is one of the ghosts of history, piqued the curiosity of the writer to find out more about him and if possible to clothe those spectral bones with flesh.

While his chief claim to a place in our history rests on his work as an educator, Jessop, like so many of our early pioneers was a man of several dimensions — the youthful adventurer making his way through wilderness, across the prairies and over the mountains to reach his new land of hope and glory; the gold seeker in the Cariboo;

the enthusiastic teacher; the unsuccessful politician and finally the Superintendent of Education creating a public school system.

His active life spanned the confederation era of British Columbia and, as we observe the centenary of British Columbia's entry into the Canadian union, it perhaps is a fitting time to revive, if only by the vicarious medium of a book, the life and times of John Jessop, the educator.

I wish to express my thanks particularly to Mr. Willard Ireland, archivist and to Miss Inez Mitchell, assistant archivist, of the British Columbia archives for their assistance in my research. To Mrs. T. H. Johns, the historian of the Metropolitan Church in Victoria I am indebted for much of the information on Jessop's church activities. I would also like to acknowledge the help given by the National Archives at Ottawa, the Ontario Archives, the archives of the Glenbow Foundation of Calgary, the Toronto Public Library, the New Brunswick Museum, the Special Collections Library at the University of British Columbia and the Northwest Room of the Vancouver Public Library. For financial help with my project I am grateful to the Research Committee of the Faculty of Graduate Studies of the University of British Columbia.

F. HENRY JOHNSON

University of British Columbia

John Jessop in later life. From the Methodist Recorder, *1901. B.C. Archives.*

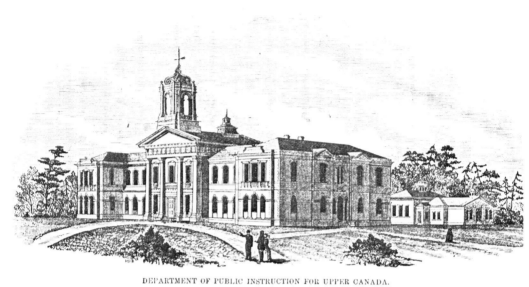

DEPARTMENT OF PUBLIC INSTRUCTION FOR UPPER CANADA.

(Education Offices First Floor to the left ; Museum Rooms up Stairs.)

The Toronto Normal School as it was when Jessop attended it. Ontario Archives.

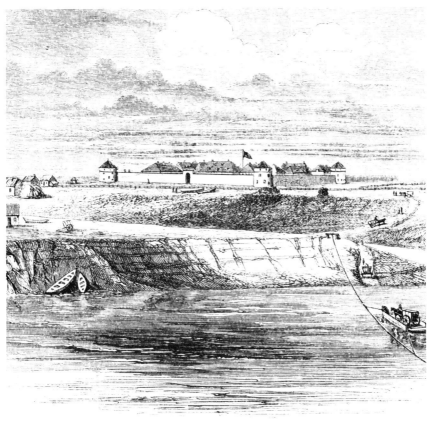

FORT GARRY.

Upper Fort Garry (Winnipeg) in 1859. From Harper's Monthly of 1861, Glenbow Archives.

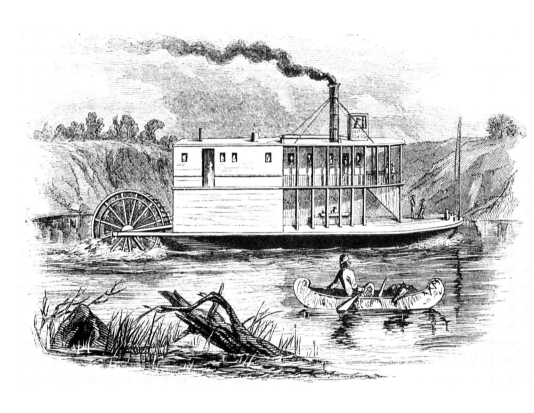

The Anson Northup, first steamboat on the Red River. Jessop witnessed its
maiden voyage in 1859. From Harper's Monthly of 1860. Glenbow Archives.

Contents

CHAPTER ONE

A Youth in Upper Canada

John Jessop was born in the old English cloth town of Norwich on June 29, 1829. His father was John Jessop and his mother's maiden name was Mary Phillippo. Here, within sight of the graceful spire of the Norman Cathedral and squat Norwich Castle he spent his boyhood years. Of the man who later was to fashion British Columbia's educational system all we know about his own schooling was that he attended "private schools",[1] presumably some preparatory school and probably a local grammar school.

In 1846 as a lad of seventeen, with his parents he joined one of the mass migrations of history— that great exodus which drained parts of the British Isles to populate North America. Hunger and desperation drove many of the emigrants; hope for a better life inspired others. Cheap passage fares in ships that had often seen better days made the voyage possible for the poorer classes who formed most of the human cargo.

"It was just as nasty as it was cheap," writes the historian Arthur Lower. "Emigrants were herded down into the holds of the oldest type of ship, those sent out to bring back cargoes of timber. Men, women and children were all mixed up together, with the most primitive of sanitary arrangements, and very limited supplies of fuel, food and water — enough water to wash in was a luxury rarely enjoyed. The stormy Western Ocean voyage might take six weeks or it might take sixteen."[2] Like so many of our forefathers, the Jessop family left no record of the reasons which motivated them to come to Canada.

They embarked on a sailing ship bound for Boston. Off the coast of Newfoundland she was struck by a fierce Atlantic gale and almost foundered. After jettisoning most of her cargo and losing a mast, spars, bulwarks and deck houses she barely managed to make the shelter of Halifax harbor. The family continued its long journey to

Upper Canada via New York and the Hudson to Watertown across Lake Ontario to Kingston and finally to Toronto.[3]

For three or four years young Jessop found work in the backwoods of Upper Canada (or Canada West as it was officially called from 1841 to 1867.)[4] He may have been employed part of this time in a newspaper office as somewhere in his early years he had learned to set type for the old hand presses. It was a skill which was to prove useful for him on later occasions when he was "down on his luck".

It was at this time, as a youth of twenty, that he joined the Methodist Church. In Upper Canada in the mid-nineteenth century the Methodists were by far the most numerous of the Protestant sects. Their itinerant saddle-bag preachers carried the fervor of their evangelism beyond the towns to the pioneer farmers and woodsmen. Perhaps it was at one of their phrenetic "camp meetings", held in Druid-like surroundings under the oaks and beeches of an Ontario glade, that young Jessop succumbed to the exhortations of the preacher and the revivalist hymns to avow his conversion to Methodism.

"The religious movement called Methodism," writes Clara Thomas in her biography of Ryerson, "was ideally suited to conditions in a new land. Phenomenally successful in eighteenth century England it was adapted perfectly to a place where there was everything to do, where most people were poor, their greatest assets strength of will and strength of body, where life was hard and good fortune chancy, but where everything was to be gained if only the effort made were great enough."[5]

It had, moreover, a peculiar affinity with education. To the Methodist the "Good Book" and the school book formed a Holy Alliance. In an almost Platonic sense, ignorance was sin and knowledge virtue. In Upper Canada at this time education and Methodism were together personified in one man — Egerton Ryerson. "The Pope of Methodism", as some of his detractors were wont to call him, was also the Superintendent of Education, busily engaged in organizing one of the finest public school systems of the nineteenth century.

Ryerson's scheme of public education did not spring from his creative imagination, nor was it a slavish copy of other countries' patterns. When first appointed to head the Public School System of Upper Canada he had straightway gone off on a fact-finding tour of Europe to glean what he could of public education policies and practices in those states which were considered most advanced in this field. He had returned to Canada, his mind crammed with good ideas

— of the latest Pestalozzian teaching methods which he had seen in Prussia and Switzerland, of Normal Schools which he had observed in Germany and Ireland, of Ireland's national system of graded textbooks, of the school laws of Massachusetts and of New York's system of financing education. All these ideas he had related to the practical needs of his own country in a lengthy report to the Canadian legislature in 1846. With this report as a blueprint, he had drafted the legislation of 1846 and 1850 which had given Upper Canada a public school system, exotic perhaps in its borrowings from other countries, but eminently indigenous and Canadian in the practical application of these ideas.

Upper Canada's public education was now systemized and centralized under a crown-nominated General Board of Education of not more than seven members who were to aid and advise an executive head, the Chief Superintendent of Education (Ryerson). The common schools were financed by provincial grants which required matching local revenues. The three-man local board might raise their share by levies (rate bills) upon only those parents who wished to send their children to school or they could levy property taxes which would then ensure "free" education for all children in the district. In many areas there was an obstinate and strong prejudice against such property taxation. Some citizens could see no reason why they should have to pay for the schooling of "every brat in the neighborhood."

It was not entirely a unified system. There were, first of all, the District Grammar Schools which had been set up as early as 1807 with public funds in the hope that they would become colonial counterparts of the English "Public" or Grammar Schools. These, however, admitted children for elementary schooling as well as for the nineteenth century classical curriculum of the traditional grammar school. Although financed generously from the public purse they could only be afforded by the socially elite as most pupils had to live in residence or lodge in the grammar school town. With their own boards, the Grammar Schools enjoyed an independence from public authority. Ryerson was striving to bring them under the authority of the General Board, to control their curriculum and the training of their masters.

The other feature which tended to mar the unity of the system was the so-called "separate school" problem. Legislation before Ryerson's accession to office had permitted Roman Catholic minority groups who wished to send their children to schools where they might have their own religious instruction, rather than the non-sectarian teaching of the public schools, to withdraw from a local school district and elect their own separate school board. These separate schools were, however, only a different kind of public school, using the provincial curricula, inspected by provincial inspectors and subject to provincial laws and regulations.

Within the many little school houses of Upper Canada, thanks to Ryerson's drive and initiative, a new broom was sweeping clean. The old "readin', writin' and 'rithmetic, taught to the tune of the hickory stick" was giving way to a broader curriculum and new teaching methods which were foreshadowing modern progressive education. Corporal punishment, that patent cure-all of the pioneer schoolmaster, was now being discouraged in favor of more positive methods of motivation such as "merit cards", "prize books" and "moral suasion." The adoption and distribution of a graded series of readers and other texts imported from Ireland was making possible a system of grading and a more homogeneous curriculum. These texts, library books, maps and other teaching aids were being purchased and made available at minimal cost to the schools by a Book Depository of the Department of Education.

But what Ryerson regarded as the chief means of reforming the schools was an institution for the professional education and training of teachers and this he had lost no time in providing. On his European tour he had particularly admired the Normal School in Dublin. To establish one such in Canada he secured the services of an able Irish educator, Thomas Jaffray Robertson, as principal. The Normal School had first opened in the old Government House of Upper Canada but in 1852 a new and splendid edifice had been built for it. A two-storied building fronted with tall pillars and crowned with a Victorian tower, it became one of the architectural show places of Toronto and until recently formed part of the complex of the Ryerson Institute of Technology.

In May, 1853, not long after the official opening of the new building, John Jessop presented himself there and was duly enrolled as a student.[6]

The teaching profession in those days was certainly not attractive from the standpoint of financial reward or social prestige. Farm laborers earned as much as most teachers, and schoolmasters were generally held in very low regard. They were commonly thought to be ne'er-do-wells and drunkards. Ryerson's ambition was to make them scholars and gentlemen by giving them the benefits of a

4

professional education, but his proposal to establish a Normal School for this purpose had been received coolly in many quarters and with open hostility in others. The original bill would have provided for "professors" at the Normal School but this was amended to read "teachers". The residents of Gore District (Hamilton) had presented a memorial in which they had stated they could see no hope "to provide qualified teachers by any other means, in the present circumstances of this country, than by securing, as heretofore, the services of those whose Physical Disabilities, from age, render this mode of obtaining a livelihood, the only one suited to their decaying energies, or by employing such of the newly-arrived emigrants, as are qualified, for Common School Teachers, year by year, as they come amongst us, and who will adopt this as a means of temporary support, until their character and abilities are known and turned to better account of themselves."

To the ardent Methodist, however, teaching was a noble work, affording an opportunity of improving the minds and morals of the young and of re-making society, and so Ryerson saw it — and so also, in all likelihood, did John Jessop.

The admission regulations of the Normal School required that candidates be at least sixteen years of age, be able to read and write intelligibly and know certain fundamentals of arithmetic.[8] Most had no more formal education than a few years in the common schools and there were at the time no written provincial examinations given for entrance to any higher level of schooling.

Jessop's formal education, aside from his training at the Normal School, had qualified him "for University Matriculation in Latin and nearly so in Greek". This was at that time the standard requirement for Grammar School teachers.[9] A certificate of moral character from a clergyman of the student's denomination was a further requirement. Jessop's was signed by a Methodist minister, the Reverend T. Robson.[10]

Most students came to the Normal School after having taught in the common schools on locally issued certificates or permits. The notation in the Training Register in Jessop's case was that he had not been a teacher before entry.[11] Some students sought admittance to the Normal School who had no intention of teaching but simply wished to improve their general education. They were admitted but without the government living allowance and were required to pay fees, but for the others who made written declarations that they intended to devote themselves to teaching there were free books and tuition and a state living allowance of a dollar a week for board and lodging.

It was Ryerson's objective to "elevate school teaching into a profession."[12] To achieve this with the young people who came to the Normal School with such inadequate backgrounds of scholarship demanded, so the Normal School authorities concluded, an almost superhuman devotion to duties. Students worked day and night with little or none of the social life usually considered necessary to youth. The regulations were stringent and almost monastic. Lectures began at nine in the morning and continued until eight in the evening with an hour break for lunch and two hours off in the afternoon. Students were required to be in their lodgings no later than nine-thirty p.m. Only "approved lodging houses, not taverns" were permitted to Normal students, all lodgings restricted to either women *or* men students.

On Saturday lectures resumed from ten-thirty until noon. Sunday was mercifully free but attendance at Divine Worship was expected.[13]

When one examines the curriculum of the school it is no wonder that the day held insufficient hours for learning. It was heavily academic in a belated attempt, no doubt, to cram into one year the high school and college education which most of these students had never had the opportunity to acquire. To modern ears its subjects sound pretentious. Surely only the most superficial acquaintance with these fields could have been attempted. What an impressive intellectual bill of fare was presented — "the Elements and Philosophy of Grammar, Orthography, Composition, Art of Reading, Rudiments of Logic, Geography, (Mathematical, Physical and Political) with rudiments of the use of the globes, Elements of General History, Linear Drawing, Mulhauser's System of Writing, Rudiments of Trigonometry, with a view to Land Surveying with the Theodolite, Art of Teaching, with daily teaching in the Model School, mode of teaching the National School Books, Science and Practice of Arithmetic, including the use of the Logarithm Tables, Algebra as far as Quadratic Equations, the Progressions, and the Binomial Theorem, inclusive; Geometry, six books of Euclid; Heat, Electricity, Galvanism, and Magnetism; Mechanics, Hydrostatics, Pneumatics, Animal and Vegetable Physiology (with special reference to the laws of health, and practical observations on the Ventilation and Temperature of School Houses), Elements of Astronomy, Agricultural Chemistry and Music."[14]

In addition to the above there was on each Friday a two-hour religious education session. It was Ryerson's belief, supported by the majority of the population, that one's education could not be complete without religious training. This should be for the regular public schools broadly Christian but non-denominational and for the Roman Catholic separate schools, of course, religious observances of that faith. The point was often made by separate school supporters and with some measure of truth, that the public schools taught a non-denominational Protestantism.

The Normal School at this time operated two sessions per year. Completion of only one permitted the student to teach on a Second Class Certificate. Completion of a second session entitled the teacher to a First Class Certificate. Jessop, probably in need of money, left in October 1853 after completing one session. He was then employed on a Second Class Certificate teaching at Darlington near Oshawa. He returned to the Normal School in May 1855 to complete his professional education graduating in October with a First Class A Certificate.[15] The "A" indicated that he stood in the upper division of his class. Jessop took what might seem to-day an inordinate pride in his First Class Teaching Certificate. In fact possessors of this qualification then were about as rare as Ph.D.'s to-day. Most common school teachers had little education and no professional training. Most grammar school teachers had more academic education, many possessing degrees from British universities, but this group scorned the thought of professional training for teaching. Moreover, the reputation of Ryerson's Normal School in Toronto stood very high not only throughout British North America but in the United Kingdom and in the United States. It was then considered to hold a position well in the van of educational progress.

In 1855 Jessop returned to teaching in Elgin County to a three-teacher school in the village of Fingal. His salary was £125 per annum "without board". Two years later we find him back in the Oshawa area teaching in Whitby in one of the new brick school houses[16] that Ryerson was encouraging the school boards to erect in place of the pioneer log shanties.

His years of teaching in Upper Canada and his professional training in the Normal School impressed Jessop most favorably with the fitness of Ryerson's educational system in all its aspects. In England he had seen nothing of a state school system. There, education of the masses was as yet left to the efforts of philanthropic church societies but here in Canada non-denominational public schools — preferably

7

free — seemed to herald a new era of democracy and opportunity.

An English traveller and writer, Mrs. Isabella Bishop, visiting in Upper Canada in the 1850's, commented on the superiority of the school system she saw: "More importance is attached generally to education in Upper Canada than might have been supposed from the extreme deficiencies of the first settlers. A national system of education, on a most liberal scale, has been organised by the Legislature, which presents in unfavourable contrast the feeble and isolated efforts made for this object by private benevolence in England."[17]

For Ryerson personally, Jessop possessed an admiration which verged on hero worship. As a student he had probably met the man and had certainly seen him and heard him speak on numerous occasions, as Ryerson's office was in a wing of the Normal School and from there the Chief Superintendent kept in very close touch with the faculty and students.

These five years of teaching in a well-respected school system gave Jessop a valuable apprenticeship and perhaps the best available model to follow when he was later in a position to create a public education system for the Pacific Province.

FOOTNOTES

[1] *The Canadian Album: Men of Canada,* Brantford, Bradley, Garretson, & Co. 1895, Vol. IV, p. 87.

[2] Lower, A. R. M. *Colony to Nation,* Toronto, Longmans Green, 1946, pp. 182, 183.

[3] Kerr, J. B., *Biographical Dictionary of Well-Known British Columbians,* Vancouver, Kerr & Begg, 1895, p. 208.

[4] "Leading Laymen". *Methodist Recorder,* Victoria, Feb. 1900, p. 9.

[5] Thomas, Clara, *Ryerson of Upper Canada,* Toronto, Ryerson Press, 1969, p. 16.

[6] Ontario Archives, Training Register of the Toronto Normal School.

[7] Hodgins, J. G., *Documentary History of Education in Upper Canada,* Toronto, Warwick, 1894-1910, Vol. VII, p. 115.

[8] *Ibid.,* VII, pp. 92, 106.

[9] Jessop to J. F. McCreight, 26 March 1872, B.C. Archives.

[10] Ont. Archives, Training Register of Toronto Normal School, 1853.

[11] *Ibid.*

[12] Hodgins, *op. cit.* VI, p. 199.

[13] *Ibid.,* VII, pp. 101, 102.

[14] *Ibid.,* VII, pp. 172, 173.

[15] Journal of Alfred Waddington, B.C. Provincial Archives, Sept. 7, 1865. Waddington, then Superintendent of the Vancouver Island Schools, listed Jessop's testimonials.

[16] Ontario Archives, Annual Reports of Local Superintendents of Schools.

[17] Quoted from Craig, G. (ed.) *Early Travellers in the Canadas,* Toronto, Macmillan, 1955, p. 214.

CHAPTER TWO

Go West, Young Man, Go West

During the 1850's Upper Canadians were becoming increasingly interested in the vast expanses of the continent that stretched to the westward. The recent Oregon Treaty of 1846 had finally established the Forty-ninth Parallel as the boundary between the United States and British territories as far as the Pacific Coast, and American families were moving in ant-like processions of covered wagons over the old Oregon Trail.

Already the Toronto *Globe* was voicing the fear that the great vacuum of the British West might next succumb to the "manifest destiny" of American expansionism. Canadians were becoming involved in Western affairs when the Imperial Government had asked the Canadian Government in 1857 to send a company of the Canadian Rifles to garrison Fort Garry when it was learned that a detachment of U.S. troops had been stationed at Pembina.[1] Pamphleteers and politicians in both Britain and Canada were already proposing railways and wagon roads from Canada to the Western plains. Upper Canadians were casting covetous eyes on the Red River settlement and the lands governed by the Hudson's Bay Company. "All sorts of dreams and speculations are floating in the public mind here," wrote Governor Sir Edmund Head to the Colonial Office, "even among sober and good men."[2]

Two expeditions of exploration launched in 1857 served to focus particular attention on the possibilities of this area, one sent out by the British Government under the command of Captain John Palliser and the other by the Canadian Government under S. J. Dawson, an engineer, and Henry Youle Hind, a science professor from the University of Toronto. Palliser's party in 1857-58 traversed the territory from Red River westward into British Columbia, examining in particular the Saskatchewan River system and the passes through the Rockies. The Dawson-Hind expedition explored particularly the water-routes from Lake Superior to Red River and westward along the Saskatchewan and its tributaries. Both expeditions reported on the suitability of the plains and parklands for agricultural settlement, Dawson and Hind being more encouraging in this regard than Palliser.

In the meantime an event occurred which suddenly accelerated for Canada the whole westward movement. This was the discovery of gold in the sandbars of the Fraser and the resulting British Columbia gold rush of '58. Into that empty land poured hordes of gold-seekers from the United States, Australia, China, Europe and Canada. The Imperial Government lost little time in creating a crown colony out of what had been the domain of the Hudson's Bay Company and in establishing therein the machinery of colonial government and British law.

To the young school teacher in Whitby, living a humdrum life with little chance of material rewards, all these reports from the West were received with the keenest interest. They quickened his pulse and the call of the Wild West with the possibility of striking it rich in the gold fields was irresistible.

"In the early spring of '59," as he related many years later, "an adventurer passed over the partly ballasted Northern Railroad from Toronto to Collingwood with knapsack, bowie-knife and a revolver (the latter of which had a knack of exploding two or three chambers at a time and was therefore condemned as somewhat unreliable, not to say dangerous) and took passage for Fort William on board a small iron steamer called the *Rescue,* on her first trip to the head of Lake Superior. After the vessel had raised the blockade at Bruce Mines by ploughing through two feet, more or less, of rotten ice in the harbour, and leaving provisions for the half-starved population, he and five or six other passengers, were landed on the ice not far from Thunder Cape and from thence made their way with all their belongings to the mouth of the Kaministiqua (sic). Two or three of these young fellows hailed from Kingston, one from Belleville and one from Paris — all being bound for Fraser River, overland, which El Dorado some of the party believed to be only a few weeks travel westward."[3]

Fort William at the mouth of the Kaministikwia had been established in 1802 as the headquarters of the old North West Fur Company because of its strategic location at the entrance to the intricate waterways to the west. Now a post of the Hudson's Bay Company, it still served as the jumping-off spot for this the only cross-country route to the Pacific. Here the little band of "overlanders" purchased a birchbark canoe, stocked up on provisions and engaged a Métis guide and an Indian steersman. After a wait of three weeks for the ice to leave the river they were off up the Kaministikwia. It was a swift stream. Two miles up they passed an Indian village with its Roman Catholic mission where some Ojibwas lived by fishing. Soon they were confronted by the "Niagara of the North" — the roaring Kakabeka Falls, 120 feet in height which Paul Kane had painted in 1846. This obstacle and a score of rapids forced them to make frequent portages or to "track" their canoe by towing it up the rapids from the bank. Ten days of hard travelling, enduring myriads of mosquitoes and "bull dog flies" brought them to Dog Lake. From here the going was easier and in a few days they reached the Savanne or Prairie Portage which was the divide between the rivers flowing east into Lake Superior and those flowing west.

Already they had consumed almost all of their Fort William stock of flour and bacon but luck was with them. After crossing the long and beautiful island-studded labyrinth of Lac des Mille Lacs, while making one of their innumerable portages, they found a bag of dried peas which some previous party had dropped. "This find proved a veritable godsend and so long as bacon lasted made a by no means despicable bill of fare. Afterwards pea soup straight twice a day — a third meal could not be afforded — was a cuisine that can hardly be recommended as a permanency."

The short but swift Maligne River required shooting or portaging half-a-dozen rapids. "To shoot rapids in a canoe is a pleasure that few Englishmen have ever enjoyed," commented George Grant of his own experiences on this river, "and no picture can give an idea of what it is. There is a fascination in the motion, as of poetry or music, which must be experienced to be understood . . . The canoe seems such a fragile thing to contend with the mad forces, into the very thick of which it has to be steered."[4] From this excitement they came out into the placid silent stretches of Lac La Croix and then Rainy Lake. At the outlet of this lake stood the Hudson's Bay Company's Fort Frances, named after the Governor Sir George Simpson's lady who once stopped here. It was a hollow square of a few buildings surrounded by a ten foot stockade with garden plots beyond. Within view was the impressive Chaudière Falls.

They had hoped that here they might replenish their larder but nothing edible could be obtained, and with heavy hearts and empty stomachs they continued on their way down the Rainy River. It was not long, however, before they came to an Indian encampment where they could purchase a supply of sturgeon — a fish which in most countries is considered a gourmet dish, but here the species did not live up to its reputation. "It was soon voted unanimously that pea soup straight was far and away preferable to the Rainy River Sturgeon with no et ceteras." Jessop related that it was many years before he could bring himself to try sturgeon again when in British Columbia. There he discovered that "the Pacific Coast sturgeon bears about the same resemblance to the Rainy or Red River article of that name as the delicious oulichan at its best does to the Eastern stickleback."

Rainy River soon brought them out on the broad expanse of Lake of the Woods. Here they followed the low rocky shores amid scrub-covered islets to the northern extremity where the lake empties into the Winnipeg River. There at the trading post of Rat Portage (now the city of Kenora) they tried to procure food but again were unsuccessful. They had no alternative but to tighten their belts and continue on their way. The Winnipeg River with its clouds of mosquitoes and gruelling portages finally came to an end and just above its outlet into Lake Winnipeg they came to Fort Alexandria where this time they were able to purchase some flour.

From here a few days travel across Lake Winnipeg and up the turgid Red River brought them to Fort Garry in June 1859.

"At Fort Garry, Fraser River seemed infinitely farther off than at the mouth of the Kaministiqua," wrote Jessop. Some members decided to go no farther and Jessop himself spent a month here. He probably needed the time to rest and recuperate for the long journey ahead. Possibly also it was to earn a little money. Of this he makes no mention in his own narrative but Gosnell who was in charge of the Legislative Library of British Columbia and who in this connection seems to have known Jessop personally, stated that "for a time" he taught school in Red River.[5]

The young Ontarian saw the Red River settlement at a most interesting period — in its sunset as a capital of a fur-trading empire and in its early dawn as a Canadian province. Palliser saw it then and described it succinctly in his report.[6] "Red River Settlement is neither a city, town, or even a village, but as the name indicates, a settlement, consisting of a straggling chain of small farm establishments, extending for a distance of forty miles along the banks, but mostly on the west bank of the Red River of the north, the dwellings being from fifty yards to a mile apart, while at intervals along this line are a few churches and windmills besides two establishments of the Hudson's Bay Company, built in the form of forts, one at the junction of the Assiniboine with the main river, and the other twenty miles below." Settlement also extended for about 25 miles westward along the Assiniboine. The total population at this time was about eleven hundred families. About half were Métis, most of these being the descendants of the French Canadian voyageurs and Indian mothers. These people were still living a semi-nomadic existence depending upon the produce of their small riverside farms supplemented by earnings as packers and by the bounty of the buffalo hunt. "They hunt during three months of the year and beg, borrow and starve during the remaining nine," wrote Palliser.

On the river bank near Winnipeg's present Fort Garry Hotel stood the stone-walled and bastioned Upper Fort Garry, the headquarters of the "Honourable Company". Here resided the Governor and here at this time were stationed the Royal Canadian Rifles. Across from the fort stood the French-speaking Métis settlement of St. Boniface with its twin-towered cathedral celebrated in Whittier's poem, *The Red River Voyageur*. Jessop too must have listened to

> The bells of the Roman Mission
> That call from their turrets twain,
> To the boatman on the river
> To the hunter on the plain!

The settlement was just beginning to foresee its importance as a transportation centre. Jessop describes how on an excursion to Lower Fort Garry he saw the first steamboat on this stretch of the Red River. "The entire population of the Selkirk settlement from Kildonan north lined the banks and gazed with wonder and astonishment upon a steamboat for the first time in their uneventful and peaceful lives." Another visitor to Red River at this time, the Scottish Earl of Southesk, described the same event in his Journal:[7]

"Thursday, the 10th of June was a notable day at Fort Garry. The first steamer that had yet navigated the Red River made her appearance that morning bringing two or three passengers from Minnesota. "Ans. Northup" was the name of this small, shabby stern-wheel boat, mean & insignificant in itself, but important as the harbinger of new developments of what Americans are pleased to call civilization. Crowds of Indians stood silently on the shore, watching the arrival of this strange portentous object."

This year saw the launching of *The Nor'-Wester,* the settlement's (and the prairies') first newspaper which in its "prospectus" noted: "Exploring parties organized under the direction, respectively, of the Canadian and British Governments have established the immediate availability for the purposes of colonization of the vast country watered by the Red River, the Assiniboine and the Saskatchewan, and private parties of American citizens following Capt. Palliser, are engaged in determining the practicability of rendering this great overland route to the gold deposits of British Columbia."[7]

In July Jessop was preparing to start across the plains. He bought an old grey horse and a Red River cart. "Neither the cart nor the harness could boast of a particle of iron or other metal in the composition, yet this motley equipage travelled with sundry repairs to the harness with buffalo thong and rawhide, fully a thousand miles to the foothills of the Rockies, and then would have rolled back again, for that matter, had it not been broken up to make primitive pack saddles". Red River carts were singularly adapted to pioneer travel on the prairies. A light box-frame poised on a maple axle connecting two large strong wooden wheels, with elm hubs, and maple rims bound with strips of raw-hide for traction, the Red River cart could be repaired wherever there was wood available. Drawn by a wiry little Indian pony and creaking and shrieking to high heaven, it could carry four or five hundred pounds for fifty or sixty miles per day. It was too light to get mired in prairie gumbo and it could be floated across rivers.

All but one of Jessop's original party had decided against proceeding farther. With this one companion, the young man from Belleville, Jessop started off on the first of August and on that day Jessop got lost. At one point on the trail to Portage La Prairie they had agreed to separate and meet later but Jessop on foot searched in vain for his companion. He spent a lonely and miserable night. "To add to the discomfort of the situation rain poured down in torrents and minus food, blankets, a fire, or the means of procuring one had fuel been within reach, the myriads of mosquitoes had what might be called a good time of it. Sunday morning came at length and the hot sun soon repaired damages to the outer man at least. On and on with nothing to eat till near noon when a strawberry patch offered some relief to the thirty-hour fast.

"South of this point, but two or three miles to the other side of a narrow lake, along which the traveller had been trudging for some time and which seemed to stretch far to the west, was a settler's house. A committee of one decided that the house must be reached by fording

Red River carts crossing the prairies. Geological Survey of Canada.

Bonaparte House near Cache Creek, the roadhouse once operated by Semlin.
Glenbow Archives.

Fort Ellice in 1859. From Harper's Monthly 1860. Glenbow Archives.

Port Douglas on the Harrison-Lillooet route to the Cariboo. From London Illustrated News. B.C. Archives.

and swimming this lake. The kind settler soon corrected the effects of long fasting and then conducted his guest back to the Portage La Prairie trail without again crossing water. Soon a speck appeared on the eastern horizon which developed speedily into a white horse and cart and a satisfactory reunion. Each had thought the other behind."

Reaching Portage La Prairie the travellers found it consisted at this time of little else than a small mission house and a Solteau Indian encampment. Plodding onward now through undulating and partly wooded country they reached Fort Ellice, a Hudson's Bay trading post on the Assiniboine about five miles below its junction with the Qu'Appelle. It had been built in 1831 and had been an important gathering point for the Métis in their great buffalo hunts. It was now chiefly important as a supply station where pemmican and dried buffalo meat were obtainable. Pemmican, one of Canada's few indigenous dishes, constituted the "iron rations" of the western traveller. It was made by pounding dried buffalo meat into small pieces, mixing it with an equal quantity of the fat and then packing it into buffalo skin bags which usually held about ninety pounds. In making the dried buffalo meat the Indian or Métis women cut the flesh into thin strips about two feet by fifteen inches wide, then smoked it over a slow fire and finally packed it in sixty-pound bales. It is doubtful if Canadian restaurants will ever feature it on their gourmet menus.

At Fort Ellice Jessop and his companion joined forces with a party of six Americans who started for the Pacific Coast from St. Paul, Minnesota, but in searching for the Yellowstone River had miscalculated their route and wandered to the banks of the Assiniboine. Stocking up on pemmican and dried meat the party of eight set off for the west in the direction of the South Saskatchewan.

They were soon marching through a hunter's paradise. Ducks and prairie chicken fell to their guns and fleet antelope bounded away from them through the tall prairie grass. It was buffalo country. "From this time on for five or six weeks and over an area of probably six hundred miles, not a clear day passed without seeing from ten or a dozen to as many as thousands or more of these noble animals . . . In these buffalo ranges then extending from a hundred miles east of the Saskatchewan Elbow to beneath the shadow of the Rockies the question of commissariat was never discussed. Buffalo heifer formed the staple, with now and then a calf, varied with plenty of antelope. Vegetables were only a memory, and the little Red River flour in stock was carefully stowed away with all that was left of pemmican for mountain provender. For a few weeks both man and beast lived literally and figuratively on the fat of the land."

Packs of vicious-looking prairie wolves followed closely on the heels of the party and fed on its refuse. "On one occasion two buffaloes were killed about half a mile from camp in the dusk of the evening and left with the intention of taking what was needed of them next morning. The dead animals, however, brought hundreds of those prairie scavengers from all points of the compass, and the pandemonium thus created can scarcely be imagined. At daylight not an ounce of flesh was to be found, while thoroughly picked bones were scattered over an acre or two of ground. Among these bones were the half devoured remains of several wolves that were killed in the frightful scramble for buffalo meat."

The country now became more arid. The party had reached that region which Palliser had considered a desert incapable of producing crops. South of the junction of the Bow and Belly Rivers they encountered sand dunes, and water supply became a problem. At this point one of the party, a stalwart Missourian, accidentally shot himself in the hand and neck, just grazing the jugular vein. Both wounds were bound up by his companions "but not before bleeding and thirst had rendered the poor fellow delirious. A little rain water caught in blankets, not of the cleanest, partially quenched his thirst. It goes without saying that there was little or no sleep in camp that night."

The next day the party made for the river, the wounded man, still delirious, strapped down in a cart and suffering agonies riding over the rough trail. However, in a few days he had recovered from his wounds and was on his feet again. By mid-September their journey across the plains was almost ended and daily they were expecting to see the Rockies.

The weather was getting chilly and foggy with occasional rain, necessitating the use of the compass in travelling, but one fine morning, as the sun cleared the mist, they gazed across the plains at one of the most marvellous sights of nature — the long line of what La Verendrye had called "the Shining Mountains." "For an immense distance the great continental backbone was plainly visible. The loftier peaks were obscured by fleecy clouds but the entire range almost down to the foothills presented an object of dazzling white." In the clear prairie air the mountains seemed only a day's march away but progress towards them was so slowed by ravines and water courses requiring many detours that it was the end of September before the party was camped in the foothills wondering now where to pierce the great barrier.

At this point, in Alberta's southwest corner, they encountered a band of Blackfeet, the "Arabs of the Canadian West," the braves splendidly mounted, bedecked in bright blankets and buckskins, their hair worn in long twin braids. Straggling behind were their women and children. At this time the Blackfeet were a proud and independent people still able to subsist as nomadic hunters following the buffalo herds. They proved to be friendly and when the overlanders told them of their desire to find a pass through the mountains to the Pacific Coast, the Blackfeet introduced one of their party who was a Kootenay Indian on his way back to his people who lived west of the mountains on the Tobacco Plains (the region where the south-flowing Kootenay River crossed the Forty-ninth Parallel). For a present of some blankets, clothing, ammunition, a rifle and some tobacco the Kootenay agreed to guide them through the Rockies. "This most providential event," in Jessop's words, no doubt saved their lives.

Before starting through the mountains the party dismantled the Red River carts to make pack-saddles for the sturdy ponies. Then "this cavalcade of tattered and dilapidated whites, and well-dressed, splendidly mounted and stalwart Blackfeet went in a north-west direction and at the end of the day's march met a much larger band with their winter's supply of buffalo meat, consisting in all of some fourteen or fifteen lodges. Next morning the white man's horses could nowhere be found. After several hours unsuccessful hunt a reward of clothing, etc., that were very much needed in view of approaching winter secured the animals in short order. They had simply been cached with this object in mind by a few of the young bucks."

The next morning they parted company with the Blackfeet and, led by their Kootenay guide, went into the mountains in the direction of what was then called the Boundary Pass. This is known today as the South Kootenay Pass. It begins in Canadian territory at the northern end of Waterton Lake and comes out in the west just south of the international boundary. The first reported crossing of this pass was made by Lieutenant Thomas Blakiston, R.A., a member of the Palliser expedition.[9] In 1858 he had taken a small party westward through the Kootenay Pass which is just south of the Crows Nest Pass and had turned south exploring the Kootenay Valley to the Tobacco Plains. Here he was told by the Kootenay Indians of the Boundary Pass which they used because it had gentler grades than the more northerly passes, and thus was easier on heavily laden horses. He had chosen to return to the prairies by this route. While his report on the pass was not in print until the year after Jessop's journey, it is entirely possible that Jessop and his party may have heard the account from people at Fort Garry or Fort Ellice and chose to try this pass in preference to others. (The Overlanders who came later in the 'sixties followed the more northerly passes through the Rockies.)

"The trail," as Jessop described it, "lay on the north side of a rippling stream with park-like grassy terraces on either side.[10] A great relief was experienced in the change from almost interminable prairie, with weeks of travelling without trees or shrubs, into open timber and plentiful wood for camp fires. On the morning of the third or fourth day in the mountains the party left a large-sized millstream and commenced some steep zigzag climbing. Unfortunately the day was cloudy so that summits were obscured. The height attained, however, was a long way short of the snow-line, as none was visible for thousands of feet above the highest point reached. In about four hours the divide was passed,[11] and a slight snow storm coming on, camp was made on a stream equally as large, with the water rushing west to the Pacific as the one left in the morning, which was hurrying away on its 2000-mile trip to Hudson's Bay. Six days of charming weather and the guide's contract ended nearly seven miles south of the line as fixed by observation a few weeks previously." This would seem to have been only the second occasion when white men had negotiated this pass although J. N. Wallace observed that, "It is an interesting question whether the first white man to have crossed some of these southern passes may not really have been Hugh Monroe who was one of the builders of Old Bow Fort and who later became a wanderer with the southern Indians."[12] The Kootenays, of course, from time immemorial had used it for access to the great plains, the home of the bison hordes.

They had arrived at a miserable little log cabin trading post of the Hudson's Bay Company known as "Fort Kootenai", situated about five miles south of the international boundary on the bank of the Kootenay River. Blakiston the previous year had described the post as "three diminutive log houses. Two of them not over ten feet square, and to enter which it was necessary to crawl through a hole as an apology for a door. These had evidently been used for dwellings; the other, somewhat larger, without a chimney, we were informed was the

Kootenai chapel which had been erected the previous spring when a priest was there."[13] Here, Jessop relates, "a canny Scotsman greeted the travellers with hearty good will and we negotiated a purchase of grizzly bear meat and berries which were all that could be obtained at the Hudson's Bay Company log cabin trading post in his charge in the shape of provisions."

This area of the Kootenay Valley was known as the Tobacco Plains. Blakiston had described it as largely prairie lands with sandy soil, covered with grass "which does not grow close and thick but in small bunches with bare ground between" — the "bunch grass" typical of the interior plateau of British Columbia and Washington. It was the home of the Kootenay Indians whom Palliser had described as "the most wretched-looking fellows I ever met; men, women and children, all living on berries, the men naked, and the women nearly so; yet strange to say, although these people were starving and destitute of clothes and ammunition, they possessed a wonderful number of horses and those very superior to the Indian horses on the east of the mountains."[14]

From Fort Kootenai Jessop's party followed "an indistinct and seldom used Indian trail" in the direction of Fort Colville on the Columbia. This trail followed the loop of the Kootenay River necessitating two crossings of this stream. The first they made by unloading their horses and rafting their packs across in a snowstorm. They then hauled their horses across by ropes. The second crossing was made without difficulty by securing the help of an Indian with a canoe. The trail left the Kootenay and crossed to the Pend Oreille. There the party divided, four following the Pend Oreille to the Columbia at Fort Sheppard, and Jessop and the other three choosing a more southerly route — through the Coeur d'Alene Mountains and valley to the Spokane River. Their supplies were almost exhausted. At the Roman Catholic mission on the Spokane the missionary was away and no food could be obtained there. The stream itself yielded "only a dozen or so small bony fish". When time was precious, a day had to be lost hunting two ponies that had strayed near Spokane Falls. The next evening they reached a newly constructed military road running from the Spokane northwest to the American settlement of Colville. One of the party found a few dried salmon skins at a recent Indian encampment and this gave them strength to continue through to Colville. The next day Jessop, now on his own, reached a settler's house "more dead than alive". Here "a hearty meal of newly baked bread and rashers of bacon" soon revived him.

At Colville Jessop learned that a pack train was preparing to leave the following day from Fort Colville (some twenty miles distant on the Columbia). Its destination was to be the Similkameen mines. He plodded on through almost zero weather to reach Fort Colville on November 5 (Guy Fawkes Day, as he commented). Here he learned that weather conditions had set in which made the Similkameen route impossible.

He was now almost at the end of his resources. His ragged appearance was the occasion for some merriment and jokes from the American troops stationed at Fort Colville. "One of the 'boys in blue' wanted to know who the overlander's hatter was, for nothing was left but the rim of what was a decent piece of headgear six months previously. Another was anxious to ascertain where his boots were made, as his only pedal protections were rawhide moccasions of his own manufacture. A third was interested in the garment that had once been a pair of tweed pantaloons, but of which nothing was left below the knee and indeed not very much above. A couple of shirts then doing duty were minus sleeves. The front and back of the vest were fastened with buffalo thong. Coat wanting, having been long since traded off to an Indian for something to eat. An old Scotch plaid over all did yeoman's service as a protection against almost zero weather."

The record of the last lap of Jessop's journey is very sketchy. Presumably he stayed long enough at Fort Colville to recuperate and to purchase clothing and further supplies. All we know is that he made the remainder of his overland journey to Fort Vancouver by land, "as the Columbia was frozen solid down to Vancouver, Washington." "With few settlers en route, and bad roads, or no roads at all, it was anything but agreeable."[15]

He reached the former Hudson's Bay Company fort which was now Vancouver, Washington, in December. Here he would have learned that steamboats and sailing ships made regular crossings to Victoria from Port Townsend on Puget Sound. Presumably he made his way northward to this port and embarked on a ship which brought him to Victoria, his future home, on New Year's Day of 1860. It had been eight weary months since he had set off from Toronto.

FOOTNOTES

[1] Morton, A. S., *A History of the Canadian West to 1870-71,* Toronto, Thos. Nelson & Sons, p. 828.

[2] *Ibid.,* pp. 825-827.

[3] Jessop, John, "Over the Plains in '58", Victoria *Colonist,* Jan. 1, 1890, p. 3. Most of the narrative that follows is from this source. (Although the *Colonist* was called the *British Colonist* and *Daily Colonist* at different times, hereinafter it will be referred to as the *Colonist.)*
Bruce Mines was a copper mining center about 50 mies east of Sault Ste. Marie on the north shore of Lake Huron.

[4] Grant, George M., *Ocean to Ocean,* Toronto, Belford, 1877, p. 53.

[5] Gosnell, R. E. *The Year Book of British Columbia,* Victoria, 1911, published by authority of the Legislative Assembly, p. 18.

[6] Palliser, J. *Papers Relative to the Exploration of British North America,* London, Queens Printer, 1859, 60, p. 54.

[7] Southesk, Earl of, *Saskatchewan & The Rocky Mountains,* Edmonton, M. G. Hurtig, 1969, p. 34.

[8] *Nor'-Wester,* Dec. 17, 1859.

[9] Palliser, J., *op. cit.,* Appendix II.

[10] Probably the Waterton River.

[11] Blakiston's barometric reading at this point was 6030 ft.

[12] Wallace, J. N., "The Passes of the Rocky Mountains Along the Alberta Boundary," Historical Society of Calgary, 1927, p. 6.

[13] Palliser, *op. cit.,* p. 72.

[14] Palliser, John, "Progress of the British North American Exploring Expedition Under the Command of Captain John Palliser, FRGS." in *Proceedings of the Royal Geographical Society 1860,* p. 291.

[15] *The Canadian Album: Men of Canada,* Brantford, Bradley, Garretson & Co., 1895, p. 87.

CHAPTER THREE

Unsuccessful Ventures

January was not perhaps the best time of the year for first impressions of Victoria but even then the beauty of the place must have affected Jessop as his ship steered its course through the narrow harbor mouth to enter a tranquil inlet. Round about low shores sloped to gently rolling hills with higher mountains to the north. Here and there were rocky outcroppings, clumps of the twisted garry oaks[1] and in the distance pine-covered hills. The inner harbor branched to the east into a short backwater, James Bay, terminating in mud flats. To the north the inlet extended a long narrow arm. The town clustered along the eastern shore at the right angle between James Bay and the northern arm. South of James Bay, across a wooden bridge lay the substantial residences of Governor Douglas, Dr. Helmcken, John Work and others of the earlier settlers. Where the present imposing Parliament Buildings stand the Colonial Council was then erecting a cluster of modest brick and timber structures nicknamed the "Bird-cages" which served the colony (and province) as its parliament buildings until 1898.

The town itself was less prepossessing in appearance than its setting, so beautifully endowed by nature. It was composed of a nondescript collection of frame buildings, relieved by a few more substantial brick edifices centred around the original Hudson's Bay Company fort, which in 1860 was still intact with its log palisade, bell-tower and bastions. Its main gate opened onto Government Street at the corner of Fort. Compared with the jerry-built shops, each with its covered porch, and the unpainted frame cottages, the H.B.C. buildings inside the palisade were still solid and imposing with their squared-log construction, neat and bright with whitewash. Beyond the few blocks of a commercial district stretched a little suburbia of shacks and tents where transients bound to and from the gold diggings made their temporary homes. Wharf Street was lined with warehouses and wharves where paddle wheel steamboats and sailing sloops were discharging cargo or preparing to leave for the Fraser River. Across the north arm facing the town was the Songhees' Indian village — a line of large flat-roofed Indian community houses made of adze-hewn cedar boards greyed by age and the elements. Blue wisps of wood smoke rose from a central hole in the roof of each. Drawn up on the beach in front of them was a line of black, gracefully-prowed dug-out canoes. North of the Songhee village was a scattering of tents and canoes of Indian visitors from "up-Island" and "up the coast" who had come to Victoria to barter their furs for food, clothing and whisky.

Accommodation for the traveller, particularly for one whose funds by now must have been almost exhausted, was not of the best. There were several hotels, the Columbia (the largest), the Colonial and the Royal. Some were of brick but none boasted a bath. Jessop may have had to settle for something similar to that described by Byron Johnson, another traveller in Victoria at this time. "I was not a little surprised on asking in the conventional manner for a bed at night to be shown by the energetic proprietor (in his shirt-sleeves, ready for any emergency) into a billiard saloon, upon the floor of which he kindly pointed out a space of about three feet wide where I might, in company with forty or fifty others, spread my own blankets and sleep upon them for a trifling fee of fifty cents."[2]

Jessop remained in Victoria during the winter months. It was no time of the year to set off for the diggings in the British Columbia interior where the severe winters had forced miners to close down their operations or to bide their time until the spring in cutting lumber for their flumes. Many returned to winter amid the fleshpots of Victoria where they could spend their gold dust more quickly than they had gained it in the town's saloons, gambling establishments and pool halls.

According to one source,[3] Jessop tried to find temporary employment as a teacher. There were at the time several private schools struggling for an existence. He would have noted the advertisement in the *Colonist* that a Mr. E. Mallandaine, architect, was opening a "Select School" on Broad Street for "children of both sexes" who were promised an intellectual menu of "English and French, drawing, mensuration, algebra, architecture and design — Evening school also from 4 to 7 p.m."[4] The Sisters of St. Ann had just opened a girls' school in a rented building on Broad Street to house their classes that had overcrowded the original log-cabin convent and school.[5] The Government maintained two "Colonial Schools" (i.e., for the children of colonists), the Victoria School at Minies' Plain beyond the eastern edge of the town and the other at Maple Point near the head of the harbor's northern arm. It served the children of the agricultural colony of Craigflower. Only the Government of the Colony made appointments to the Colonial Schools and there were evidently no temporary positions open in private schools.

In all likelihood Jessop may have found work in another field in which he had had experience, that is, as a newspaper man. The *British Colonist* had been founded just over a year previously by a Nova Scotian photographer who had changed his name from William Alexander Smith to the more resounding Amor de Cosmos. A tall blackbearded Don Quixote, he was already tilting his editor's pen at the powers that be — Governor Douglas and the "Family-Company-Compact" that ruled the small colony. A Government Gazette was also being published at this time. Its editor was an Irishman, Leonard McClure. In view of Jessop's later association with McClure, it is very likely that he may have worked on the Gazette at this time.

However or wherever he was employed during those winter months he managed to exist and to see something of the colorful and varied life of this little capital. The hectic gold rush of 1858 had slackened to some extent by now but miners and colonists were still pouring in to the town. It was a free port, the depot for all supplies moving into the interior. Its population in 1860 was transient but estimated at between two and three thousand. In February the *Colonist* announced that "a census taken in the last three days" showed the total number of inhabitants "exclusive of Indians and sailors on board vessels in the harbor is 2020. This includes fifty soldiers quartered at the Government House, prisoners in jail and the police force."[6] It was a population drawn from every corner of the earth — Americans in large numbers, a little British élite, from Europe — Germans, French, Italians, Spaniards, Scandinavians, Poles and Russians. There were negroes seeking freedom from the slave states, Mexicans, Lascar seamen from Goa, Kanakas from the South Seas deserting their ships to try their luck in the gold fields, Chileans and Malays and Chinese in their hundreds. Many of the merchants and real estate agents in town were Jewish who had moved in from San Francisco and other American cities. Much of the manual labor was done by the Indians, who too often spent their earnings on liquor.

On Government, Wharf and Fort Streets the merchants did a thriving business catering to the motley crowd that lounged about the wooden sidewalks and loitered on the porches of the saloons, hotels, restaurants and fashionable shops. There seemed to be a demand for everything from whisky and miners' tools to the latest in London fashions as advertised for sale at Mr. Nathan Pointer's emporium. "A beautiful lot of Gentlemen's Dressing Robes also a magnificent assortment of Silk Umbrellas of high finish. A full assortment of Gent's Superfine White Shirts. A new style of Byron Collars and Garrote Collars, the latest styles of Imperial Cravats."[7]

"The average Victorian's sense of bliss," wrote one contemporary pioneer, "apparently consists of the largest possible number of drinks in the shortest possible time, varied with cigars and billiards ad. lib."[8] Jessop's Methodism would doubtless have directed him into channels of entertainment more in conformity with the tenets of mid-Victorian respectability. Perhaps his was one of the faces in the crowd that filled the Royal Theatre one night in January to see the Chapmans, a travelling family of Thespians, perform "The Stranger". It was "finely rendered," according to the *Colonist*. He probably took advantage of one of the free lectures advertised in that worthy paper. Surely he would not have missed hearing the Rev. W. F. Clarke in the Congregational Lecture Room on "The Perils of the Search for Gold".[9] His interests also might have taken him to the Burns Dinner held on January 25 in the Colonial Hotel where the memory of the immortal Scot was toasted in his native beverage by the Scots-in-heart on that far-distant shore. On Sundays he would have attended the Methodist services which were then being held, pending the erection of a church, in the new brick Police Building on View Street.

The previous summer the gold-seekers had moved north from the lower to the upper Fraser and a thousand of them were working the stretch from Alexandria to Fort George.[10] On July 15, 1859 the *Colonist* had reported the discovery of gold in the gravel of the Quesnel River. Now as the days lengthened into a promise of spring Jessop watched the *Colonist's* reports from the diggings in the upper country and talked with men who had returned from there. On his walks down to the waterfront he would watch miners at work building their flat-bottomed boats to take them across Georgia Strait to the Fraser River.

Preparations for departure came at last and Jessop was ready with other adventurers to set off for the interior. One eye-witness left a vivid account of just such a scene. "Criers paraded the streets, shouting forth the hours of departure of various steamboats for New Westminster (the capital of British Columbia and the next place on the way to the mines) and the fares, which latter, as there was considerable competition, were very low. Parties of sober miners, clad in blue or red shirts, with their pants tucked in to knee boots, their belts showing the usual jackknife and revolver, their heads crowned with wide felt hats and their backs laden with small well put-up packs consisting of a pair of blankets, enclosing a spare shirt and pair of socks (with the addition, perhaps, but not in many cases I expect from the bearer's appearance, of a piece of soap) wended their way quietly to the wharves and got on board the expectant steamers."[11]

An uneventful cruise through the lovely Gulf Islands and across the broad stretch of the strait brought them to the muddy waters of the Fraser. Here for fifteen miles they steamed past the rich alluvial lands of the delta islands to tie up finally at the little river port of New Westminster.

Commonly called "Stumpville", there was little to dignify this village as the capital of the mainland colony of British Columbia. It was situated on the slopes of a steep hill that had been selected as the site by a colonel of the Royal Engineers whose concern was for its defensibility from the wicked Americans to the south. Its main street followed the river bank and the cross streets were muddy tracks up the hillside. A hotel or two, some boarding houses, a score of stores and some pleasant little cottages along the river bank and that was it — New Westminster, "The Royal City". Beyond the stump-studded clearings rose the dense rain-forest of British Columbia. A mile up river (at what is now called Sapperton) was the encampment of the Royal Engineers, that valuable military arm which had kept order in the colony, surveyed its capital, laid out its streets and was constructing trails and roads into the interior.

The steamboat pulled in to the wharf to be greeted by a crowd of townsfolk and brightly blanketed Indians. Jessop and the miners disembarked to await another steamboat which would take them the next day up the river and to the head of Harrison Lake from which point a succession of trails and water routes led to Lillooet on the upper Fraser. The men pitched their tents on the river bank; lit the camp fires to cook their beans and bacon and turned in for the night.

The next morning the whistle of the river steamboat summoned the miners aboard. The steamers in service on the Fraser were "peculiarly

American" as Commander Mayne had called them.[12] With their stern paddle wheels "they are admirably adapted to pass between snags and close to bluffs where a side-wheel would be knocked away." With flat-bottomed hulls the vessels drew no more than two feet of water. Their bows were shovel-nosed to enable them to pull up close to the banks. The boilers were well forward near the bows and the engine room was astern so that long pipes had to conduct the steam from boiler to the cylinders from which cranks and connecting rods converted the energy to the large stern paddle wheel which was often 20 to 24 feet in diameter. Some of these paddle wheelers had been bought in the United States but Victoria had started its own ship-building industry, launching its first steamboat in 1858.[13] For many years these were the craft that serviced the lakes and rivers of British Columbia and Jessop was to know them well on his travels.

The passage up-river was slow against the swift current. The valley was beautiful, its river banks densely forested, and in the distant east the rugged snow-topped Golden Ears were visible against the sky. Where the clear water of the Harrison River joined the muddy Fraser the sternwheeler left the parent stream and followed the Harrison for a few miles to Harrison Lake. Crossing that forty-mile stretch of water surrounded by its alpine scenery they reached the north end of the lake and a small stream barely wide enough for the river boat to negotiate. A half-mile of this narrow stream led them finally into Little Harrison Lake, and crossing it they came to Port Douglas, the point of entry to the Cariboo. "There is nothing pretty in the town," wrote one traveller, "which is a row of log huts in a small clearing surrounded by the forest, with the road to the diggings perceptible up the hill behind."[14]

Two years earlier Governor Douglas had enlisted a corps of unemployed miners to cut a trail from this point north to enable the gold-seekers to get to the upper Fraser at Lillooet. Known as the Harrison - Lillooet trail it was being widened in 1860 to make a 38-mile wagon road from Port Douglas to the chain of lakes (Lillooet, Anderson and Seton) where boats were available. Short stretches of trail connected the lakes and from Seton Lake a three-mile road led to Lillooet on the Upper Fraser. For travellers in the spring of 1860 the trail was rough going, transportation on the lakes was by row boats, which were not replaced by lake steamboats until later that year. Mosquitoes were a constant nuisance. Between Douglas and Lillooet there were perhaps a dozen "mile houses" or crude log-cabin inns. Here the wayfarers might get food and drink for themselves and hay for their horses, after which they could find a place on the floor where they could roll up in their blankets and sleep free of charge. One traveller's diary after such a night read: "Slept in road house on floor with others. Bar-keeper sleeps on his counter to guard his liquor — mosquitoes bad — sore feet. Breakfast flap jacks and coffee."[15]

From the village of Lillooet Jessop crossed the Fraser to a little settlement called Parsonville or Lower Fountain. From here the trail zig-zagged steeply up four thousand feet to the summit of Pavilion Mountain and then for over 200 miles through open and pleasant country north to the Quesnel River. The beauty of this interior plateau impressed one traveller who noted in his diary:[16] "The first part of today's walk was very pleasant although it rained, and it was thoroughly English-looking; we were up among the hills on a large undulating plain with here and there a clump of trees or range of bushes and the whole covered with good green grass, which is very scarce here, the generality of the grass which covers the hills being yellow, dry and coarse . . . Roses are plentiful all over the country, right up to the Cariboo in the plains, woods and hedges . . . The trees here, especially those that fall, get covered with a beautiful greenish yellow moss which has a very pretty appearance . . . we also found Lupins growing in the wood in the greatest abundance, in leaf and flower identical with our English plant."

Weary and footsore, Jessop at last reached the banks of the Quesnel River, the scene of the most recent gold discoveries. In April the *Colonist's* correspondent here had written, "The richest and most extensive mines that have been discovered in this upper country are in the Quesnelle River, commonly called the Canal river . . . The gold taken from the Quesnelle River and its tributaries is of the coarse order and much of it resembles shot."[17] Another miner gave a less glowing account: "To one that is doing well twenty are reported as not making grub. Flour $125 per 100 lb., bacon $1.50 per lb. Tools not to be had."[18]

In this new mining area the first permanent camp to develop was at Quesnel Forks where the Quesnel River coming from the broad stretches of Quesnel Lake to the southwest was joined by its tributary, the Cariboo, curving down through Cariboo Lake from the mountains to the north. Quesnel Forks in 1860 consisted of a dozen or more stores and saloons, and a score or more of cabins and tents. Already miners were pushing beyond this point and up the Cariboo River where this spring "Doc" Keithley and J. P. Diller struck it rich on a bluff overlooking a creek which flowed into Cariboo Lake. The resulting rush to "Keithley Creek", as it came to be called, created another fly-by-night mining camp there. "Doc" Keithley mined his claim successfully for a short time and then sold out. One of the gang on Keithley Creek, George Harvey, decided to prospect up the Cariboo River and about ten miles farther on discovered another gold-bearing creek which was named after himself.[19] According to the *Colonist* one man on Harvey Creek panned seventy dollars in one day and the average yield on this creek was from eight to ten dollars a day.[20] "On Harvey's Creek men are making from eight dollars to fifty dollars per day to the hand and in some cases much more. Harvey and Company (five men) four days ago cleaned up and found that they had made $2100 for six days work of as pretty gold as ever came out of the ground! On this stream about a hundred men are at work and I think at least 30,000 feet of lumber are in use — all of which has been sawed this season by hand."[21] Jessop arrived on the scene just at this time and joined the rush to Harvey Creek.[22] But fortune eluded him here. He made another try at Keithley Creek where there were about 150 miners at work. Here, like the others, he constructed a flume, made himself a crude "rocker" and washed the gravel. It was hard work and the "pay dirt" was pitifully small. He sustained himself on the usual fare of the miners, "Cariboo turkey" (bacon) and "Cariboo strawberries" (beans).

In the fall, when the men were still busy in the creeks in the daytime and betting their gold in the crowded gambling halls at night, Jessop decided to pull up stakes and returned to the coast.

Arrived in New Westminster after the long trek down from the Cariboo, Jessop sorely needed employment. He had a debt of $120 to pay off for the supplies he had purchased.[23] Fortunately for him he was befriended by Leonard McClure, New Westminster's first municipal leader. The town's first council had been elected in August 1860 and McClure had later been chosen "President" of it. He had lost no time in embarking on a program of clearing land, grading streets and reserving lots for schools and other public buildings. He was also the publisher of the first newspaper in New Westminster and in the colony of British Columbia. In March 1860 he had purchased *The Times,* a weekly which had begun publication in Victoria but with the object of providing news of the mainland colony and "to scan and scrutinize" every act of the British Columbia Government.[24] Its press was in Victoria. The papers were sent to New Westminster by steamer. When McClure purchased *The Times* he brought the old hand press to New Westminster. "I toiled up the steep ascent", as he related, "over logs and stumps, through brush and tangled weeds, hauling, with the aid of the unwilling savage the first printing press in British Columbia."[25] Either because Jessop had worked with him before in Victoria or learning of his experience in typesetting and newspaper work, McClure employed him on his paper. It is very likely that another of the paper's employees at this time was John Robson, also an Ontarian like Jessop, who had arrived in the colony in 1859 and who also had tried his luck unsuccessfully in mining.[26]

McClure, however, was having financial troubles and in late January of 1861 he had to sell the paper to a group of New Westminster citizens who offered the editorship to John Robson.[27] The name of the paper was changed to the *British Columbian*. The first issue appeared February 13, 1861. As New Westminster's pioneer newspaper it has published under this name ever since. Robson found that the "power of the press" was such as to enable him to become a member of the Colonial Legislature and later premier of his province.

James Douglas, who had been appointed Governor over both Vancouver Island as well as the newer colony of British Columbia, was having considerable difficulties politically with the younger child. The New Westminster merchants complained of what to them seemed to be the dominance of Victoria and a neglect of their own welfare. Jessop seems to have been one of the leading critics of the Government at this time. Amor de Cosmos' Victoria paper, *The Colonist*, was also critical of the Douglas Government. In its issue of January 29, 1861, under the heading "Not a Government Candidate," it quoted a letter from "Mr. John Jessop of New Westminster" — too long for insertion in full — in which he took exception to being classed among the Government candidates at the Convention election. "At the nomination," Jessop wrote, "I clearly defined my position as being entirely antagonistic to the existing government and unmistakeably denounced British Columbia misrule; and I assure you, sir, that I should not have troubled you with this communication did I not consider it necessary as a comparative stranger and a British Columbian to disabuse the public mind and clear my own character of an unfounded aspersion". The editor of the *Colonist* added his own postscript: "We always thought Mr. Jessop too sensible a man to support absolutism."[28] It was Jessop's first step into the political arena where he was later to fight two unsuccessful bouts.

When the New Westminster *Times* was sold, McClure, Jessop and two compositors moved to Victoria, formed a co-partnership and started the Victoria *Press*. The first issue appeared on March 9, 1861. It was a four-page paper appearing tri-weekly at twelve cents a copy. It too had its difficulties. The editor often had to set up his articles himself for the old hand press. The paper would get to press at irregular hours in the early morning, and sometimes on colored wrapping paper if they had no funds to purchase newsprint.[29] By the summer of 1861 the *Press* was on its last legs financially and Jessop left it to start a new career.

FOOTNOTES

[1] Garry oak *(Q. Garryana Dougl.)* is the only species of oak native to British Columbia.
[2] Johnson, R. Byron, *Very Far West Indeed,* London, Sampson, Low, 1872, p. 39.
[3] Kerr, J. B. *op. cit.,* p. 207.
[4] *Colonist,* Jan. 7, 1860.
[5] Down, Mary M., *A Century of Service,* Victoria, Sisters of St. Ann, 1966, p. 49.
[6] *Colonist,* Feb. 25, 1860, p. 3.
[7] *Ibid.,* Jan. 7, 1860.
[8] Johnson, R. Bryon, *op. cit.,* p. 45.
[9] *Colonist,* Jan. 28, 1860.
[10] Elliott, Gordon R., "Quesnel, Commercial Centre of the Cariboo Gold Rush", Quesnel, *Cariboo Observer,* 1958, p. 19.
[11] Johnson, *op. cit.,* p. 50.
[12] Mayne, R. C., *Four Years in British Columbia and Vancouver Island,* London, John Murray, 1862, p. 90.
[13] Smith, Dorothy Blakey, "Harry Guillod's Journal of a Trip to the Cariboo, 1862". *B.C. Historical Quarterly,* July-Oct. 1955, p. 199.
[14] *Ibid.,* p. 199.
[15] MacFie, Matthew, *Vancouver Island and British Columbia. Their History, Resources and Prospects,* London, Longmans Green, 1865, p. 226.
[16] Smith, *op. cit.,* p. 205.
[17] *Colonist,* April 17, 1860, p. 1, "Letter from Quesnelle River".
[18] *Colonist,* May 26, 1860.
[19] Elliott, *op. cit.,* p. 22.
[20] *Colonist,* Aug. 4, 1860, p. 3.
[21] *Ibid.,* Sept. 15, 1860, p. 3.
[22] Kerr, J. B. *op. cit.,* 207.
[23] *Methodist Recorder,* Victoria, Feb. 1900, p. 9.
[24] Macdonald, Margaret Lillooet, "New Westminster 1859-1871", M.A. thesis, U.B.C., 1947, p. 391.
[25] *Ibid.,* p. 391.

[26] *Ibid.*, p. 392, and Lamb, W. K., "John Robson vs. J. K. Suter" in *B.C. Historical Quarterly,* IV, 3, July 1940, p. 205.

[27] *Colonist,* Jan. 25, 1861.

[28] *Colonist,* Jan. 29, 1861, p. 2.

[29] Kerr, J. B., *op. cit.,* p. 207. The Provincial Archives has a full file of *The Press.*

CHAPTER FOUR

Victoria Schoolmaster

In the summer of 1861 Jessop decided to return to teaching. He was thirty-two, still a young man but perhaps ready now to settle down after his travels and adventures of the past three years. He liked the country and sensed that it would have a great future. Was there a future for him in its educational system? While he enjoyed teaching, at the same time he was ambitious and an opportunist and he could not contemplate with any degree of enthusiasm spending his life in the classroom and living on the meager pittance of a schoolmaster. With his training and experience in what was then recognized as one of the outstanding public school systems in the world, he felt that there was a position of leadership which he could fill in the educational life of this new land.

At this time the children of the colony of Vancouver Island, if they went to school at all, patronized either private schools or the "Colonial Schools" which were run by the Government. The latter had been inaugurated by Governor Douglas in 1852 for the children of those settlers who had already begun to trickle in to the Island colony. By 1861 there were still only three colonial schools, one in Victoria, one at Craigflower and one in Nanaimo. These schools were administered directly by the Council of the colony. There were no local school boards. To supervise this tiny school system the Government had appointed the Colonial Chaplain, the Reverend Edward Cridge, as a part-time Honorary Superintendent of Education. On August 27, 1861 he had reported to the Government on the state of these schools.[1] The Victoria School under W. H. Burr had 56 pupils registered, only 3 of whom were girls but the average attendance was only 42. Craigflower, under H. Claypole had 23 registered, 8 of whom were girls and an average attendance of 16. The Nanaimo school taught by C. Bryant had 32 pupils registered, ten being girls. The average attendance was 24. His report was apologetic. The schools were benefitting the colony and "at a small charge on the Public revenue" but "it is plain that they are at present in an imperfect and Elementary state." This he ascribed principally to the irregularity of attendance on the part of the pupils (a responsibility of the parents) and to what he considered to be an excessively large pupil-teacher ratio.

A large segment of the population was critical of the school system. It found its *vox populi* in the fiery editor of the *Colonist,* Amor de Cosmos. Since 1859 he had been attacking the Government and its educational policy on the grounds that it was trying to set up the Church of England as a state church with "religious reserves" of public lands. When Edward Cridge had asked the Government for a renewal of his contract as Colonial Chaplain, de Cosmos had protested that "by this means we have virtually a State Church". Moreover, Cridge was also superintendent of the colonial schools and inspector of the religious education therein conducted.[2] De Cosmos was supported by religious dissenters and many others when in August 1860 he had criticized Douglas' opening speech to the Assembly for neglecting the need of a good public school system "free from denominational bias". In August 1861 Anglican Bishop Hills made an important move toward an amicable settlement of the issue when he advised his church committees to refuse any further land grants. But the schools still reflected the scriptural teachings of the Church of England; they were still under an Anglican cleric and they were not "public" in the sense that they were not free. Pupils paid fees of a pound per annum. In Victoria's private schools fees for day pupils ranged from three to five dollars a month. Teachers in the Colonial Schools received, in addition to the pupils' fees, an annual grant of £150 each. Although no figures were available for the enrolments in private schools in Victoria in 1861 it is very likely that they far exceeded the numbers attending the Colonial Schools.

Jessop was known to be critical of the British Columbia Government and of the close affiliation between Church and State in education. Very likely, therefore, he would be *persona non grata* with either Governor Douglas or Edward Cridge. Even had he desired a position in the colonial school system he realized that his chances were nil.

Consequently he opened a school of his own. "In August '61", as he subsequently described to the press, "a most urgent and pressing want was felt in the community for an entirely non-sectarian and cheaper school than any that then existed — and in order to meet that want the Central School was established."[3] It was first housed in the old Assembly Hall at the foot of View Street in, as one writer described it, "a rickety place being neither wind nor water tight."[4] He called it the Central School because it was "down town" compared with the Victoria Colonial School which was located about three hundred yards beyond the city's eastern boundary.

In both the Colonial Schools and the private schools of Vancouver Island (with the exception of the school of the Sisters of St. Ann) the English and Anglican influence was pronounced. The Colonial Schools seemed to follow the curriculum and books of the National Schools of the Church of England. When they had first been established Douglas proposed that they offer "moral and religious training and a good sound English education and nothing more."[5] The Anglican Church also had two parochial schools in Victoria, one for boys and the other for girls. In fact Cridge, assisted by his wife, operated a young ladies' boarding school in his parsonage. For most of these private schools the model, consciously or otherwise, was that of the British middle or upper class tradition. Although he had been born in England and had received his own schooling there, Jessop was, however, a great admirer of the Upper Canadian public school system of Ryerson, for which he had been trained as a teacher and in which he had taught. He intended to operate his own school on these same principles.

Shortly after his school was opened he sent off a letter to Dr. Egerton Ryerson which throws an interesting light on Jessop's plans and character.[6] It reveals him as a far-sighted young man who now had a clear purpose in life. It was the first step in establishing a new cultural liaison between this predominantly British colony and the school system of Canada. Under Jessop's influence this bond was to grow stronger with the years.

> Victoria, V.I.
> August 16th 1861.

Rev. E. Ryerson, D.D.
   Chief Supt. of Schools &c, &c
      Rev. Sir

Having, at the solicitation of many of the citizens of Victoria, commenced a school and believing that a good opening presents itself for introducing the system of which you are the Honored Head, and under which I received my training during two sessions at the Provincial Normal School and more than five years as a common School teacher in different parts of

Canada West, I am desirous of making it as efficient as possible and for that reason I have taken the opportunity of applying to you, through an old friend D. Ormiston B.A., for a supply of maps, charts, apparatus &c, &c, for the use of the school and for the benefit of the city of Victoria.

Our Common School here is very inefficient, while two others, one under the control of Bishop Hills of the Established Church, and another for Young Ladies in charge of the Sisters of Mercy have so much of the Sectarian element in their government as to make them distasteful to non-conformists of all denominations. A school, therefore started and conducted exclusively on non-sectarian principles, as the one under my charge is and will be, and moreover carried on according to the admirable system of Canada West, cannot fail of soon becoming popular and flourishing. My object is to establish its reputation, and when the city is incorporated to fall in with the common school system that will then be adopted, and place myself at the head of the common schools of Victoria and Vancouver Island.

I believe I am the only person in the Island or in British Columbia that holds a first class Provincial certificate, or indeed one of any description from the Normal School. I have therefore a good opportunity in my present position to do a great deal toward placing the common school system here on a satisfactory basis.

I feel convinced you will, if possible, aid me in establishing an efficient school by sending from the Educational Department a good selection of Maps, charts, globes, phylosophical and chemical apparatus &c, &c, on the terms you supply them to schools under the control of your Department.

I have written to Mr. D. Ormiston who with his estimable brother the Rev. Dr. Ormiston will I am sure interest themselves in anything pertaining to my success and advancement in life, on the subject and I have no doubt the requisite amount of funds for such a purpose will be advanced by either of those gentlemen.

I am desirous of obtaining this supply with as little delay as possible and for that reason would prefer having them shipped from New York per steamer for San Francisco as slow freight rather than sent round the Horn in a sailing vessel at a lower rate of freight, as the transit by way of the Isthmus would be at least three months quicker than the other mode of conveyance.

The Rev. Dr. Evans very kindly encloses a note to you as a guarantee of good faith on my part in making this application.

My address is, John Jessop Central School Victoria Vancouver Island, *Via* New York, Panama and San Francisco.

I have the honor to be
Rev Sir,
Your most obt. Servt.,
John Jessop

According to a pencilled note on the letter, Ryerson wrote a reply on October 3, 1861, which regrettably has been lost. It would be interesting to know whether he did agree to supply Jessop in his new school with the textbooks and teaching aids prepared for the schools of Upper Canada.

Jessop's schools got off to a very successful start the first year with seventy-five pupils enrolled. To compete with the low fees of the Colonial Schools and to enable students to attend who could not pay the high fees of other private schools he set the Central Schools fees so low that he cleared scarcely more than a hundred dollars per month over expenses.[7]

At Christmas 1861 Jessop staged his first "public examination." Nothing is more redolent of the Victorian era in Canadian education than the custom of the public examination. It was held at least once a year and often twice with the two-fold purpose of giving parents the chance to see their young offspring in action and of affording the teacher an opportunity to display the prowess of his pupils. It was by no means an ordinary day in school. Everything was rehearsed to the perfection of a music festival. The school room was tidied up and decorated with displays of the children's handwriting and art work. The children were well scrubbed and dressed in their "Sunday best". To parents and children (but not to the teachers) it was one of the chief forms of entertainment and excitement in the quiet Victorian age. The *Colonist* reported: "We were present a short time yesterday at the examination of Mr. Jessop's school. About 50 scholars and a goodly number of grown persons were present. The examination was in every aspect satisfactory. The school is growing daily and the favourable result of yesterday's proceedings cannot fail to add to its number of pupils."[8]

As soon as he had his first class enrolled Jessop made plans to vacate the drafty old Assembly Hall and erect a school of his own at a cost of $3,000. It was situated on Fort Street between Douglas and Blanshard.[9] According to the *Colonist* reporter it was "the largest building in the city consecrated to the service of education. It is built of wood and plastered within and is two stories high. Its front elevation on Fort Street is fully 30 feet wide by 50 feet in depth, with yards behind nearly 70 feet long. The interior is extremely well arranged for holding classes—and the air of neatness and cleanliness observable about the premises is cheering to behold". Over the two small rooms at the entrance was a gallery and at the rear a second gallery. The large central space between was the classroom fitted with desks. On the walls were mounted blackboards, "educational maps of the four quarters of the globe, and several anatomical figures." The yard had certain unusual features. There was a wooden floor at a slight incline to drain off water so that children could play there without getting muddy. A fence divided the yard into the boys' and girls' sections and these were remarkably well provided with gymnastic equipment—swings, parallel bars, climbing ladders, tumbling bars, rings, and even merry-go-rounds.[10] Central School was the last word in what Jessop thought the well-equipped school should be.

Before the school reopened for the second term in August 1862 he had also added to his staff, anticipating a heavy enrolment. He appointed as his assistant D. B. Chisholm, "late of Oakville, Canada West, where he was for many years in charge of a flourishing school." "Mr. C." announced the *Colonist,* "is a gentleman of ability and a real worker — one of the few immigrants who have blistered their hands by honest labor since their arrival in this colony. Men of his stamp are a valuable acquisition to a new country."[11]

The services of a French lady, Mme. Pettibeau, were secured to teach some of the girls the tongue of Molière and the gentle art of "fancy work." She conducted her little class in one of the galleries; the principal took a class of boys in the other and Mr. Chisholm held forth in the large classroom below.

When Christmas came around again and the parents and press were once more invited to the public examination the *Colonist* was loud in its praises of the school, its building, its teachers, the progress of the pupils and its curriculum.[12] "The course of instruction embraces a wide field of study — but the comparative youth of the children generally renders the most elementary training necessary here, as well as in the other schools of the colony. The closing exercises, yesterday, were specially designed to show the parents and those interested in education the modes of teaching and the progress of the tutored and we regretted that the attendance was so limited to witness what to our minds conclusively proved the entire success which crowned the wearisome and

40

laborious duties of the principal and his assistants. The children looked exceedingly cheerful and happy, proving that their teachers are not monsters in their youthful imagination as we regret to say is too often the case, and the promptness with which they answered the questions put to them evinced an intelligent perception of their nature highly creditable to the little ones themselves and not less so to their skilful mentors. In singing the children seem to have made great progress . . . We should judge that this is really a model school . . . Before the school was dismissed an incident occurred which strikingly evinced the love and respect which the pupils have for Mr. Jessop. The girls had previously subscribed among themselves and bought a neat gold pencil-case which they presented to him before taking their leave for the holidays."

That second year the enrolment was about a hundred day pupils, in addition to which Jessop carried on night classes for adults. He had built his new school and expanded his staff on the assumption that the enrolment would continue to grow at a satisfactory rate. There were reports also of numerous families on their way to the colony from England.[13] However, when he came to open his school for the third year in August 1863 only fifty pupils came. Jessop was dismayed. His plans were in ruins, his hopes dashed. He could not pay his two assistants and regretfully had to let them go. He worried about paying off his debts on the building. In a black mood he dashed off a long letter to the *Colonist* venting his spleen against an unappreciative and callous public. He had provided the city with a large, well-equipped school run on the most modern and approved lines and offering a good, completely non-sectarian education for their children — and to his chagrin, the public had not supported it. "The public has been designated an 'ungrateful monster', and truly I think the assertion is correct." Had he "all along occupied some dingy, uncomfortable, ill-ventilated old barrack, with seats without backs, and so high that the feet of the pupils would dangle in mid air, instead of the admirably adapted and roomy building . . . with its gymnasium and everything else to make it agreeable" he would have saved himself much trouble and financial loss. "The inestimable blessing of 'a sound mind in a sound body' does not appear to be appreciated by the mass of the community."

He concluded his letter, somewhat prophetically, by saying that "nothing but the hope that ere long something of an educational system will be inaugurated and that the public common schools will soon be permanently established, keeps me in the thankless position of a teacher and enables me to bear up under such a complication of difficulties."[14]

In mentioning the need for establishing a good public school system for the colony, Jessop was referring to the increasing criticisms of the Colonial School system as administered by the Reverend Mr. Cridge. It was not free; it was not non-sectarian; the Victoria school was greatly overcrowded and not conveniently located for most of the city children. There was no central board or authority for the colony concerned solely with the advancement of education and no local school boards. For every four children attending the Colonial Schools there were eleven enrolled in other private and church schools regardless of the higher fees.[15]

Amor de Cosmos had been using the editorial columns in his *Colonist* to promote the idea of a free non-sectarian school system and educational reform. In April 1862 he had proposed the creation of a Board of Education for the colony and locally elected school trustees following Canadian practice.[16] Jessop knew that there were many prominent Victorians who shared this desire to see a good free common school system established and that it could be achieved if the public were sufficiently aroused.

The action he took in the spring of 1864 was just what was needed. He determined to close the Central School and sell the premises and equipment. The *Colonist* commented: "Mr. Jessop, the well known principal of the Central School, Fort Street, has determined, on account of ill health, to break up his establishment. The school has long been a popular institution with a large class of the community and its closing will leave a blank among the education facilities of the city which will be deeply felt."[17]

In the *Colonist* of April 1, a notice appeared that "The well-known and desirable property called the Central School. Fort St." was to be put up for "Peremptory Sale" and that if not used for a school building it was "admirably adapted for a small church, Council Chambers and Town Hall or Temperance Hall." The same issue of the paper contained the report of the final public examination of the pupils of the Central School: "Mr. Jessop addressed the scholars in a very pathetic manner, explaining the reasons for giving up the school and expressing his regret that some notice had not been taken by the proper authorities to establish a common school within the city. He said that as a private school, under his management, that day finished his career. Should, however, a common school be started, he would be happy if his services were accepted, to meet them again in the position of teacher."[18] To the prominent Victorians assembled for the occasion and to the reading public the point was made — and it was a point with a purpose.

Jessop was well aware of the popular concern over the school situation. He knew that there were many of the better off and particularly supporters of the Church of England and its schools who were satisfied with the status quo but that there were increasingly more settlers, and particularly the non-conformists like himself, who wanted free and non-sectarian schools. Also he could not have been ignorant of recent political developments in the school situation. Governor Douglas had just retired and in March the new Governor of Vancouver Island, Arthur Edward Kennedy had arrived in Victoria where, for lack of a Governor's residence and the civil list that he felt should go with it, he had to settle his family and himself in the St. George's Hotel. A kindly and none-too-tactful Irishman, Kennedy was known to favor non-sectarian schools. Moreover, a committee of the House of Assembly under the chairmanship of James Duncan had been appointed to look into the schools issue. After considerable delay its report was completed on March 18 but had not yet been made public.

On April 8 the *Colonist* carried two items which again show Jessop's opportunism and sense of timing. Mr. Selim Franklin, a member of the House of Assembly, had given notice of motion to amend the Incorporation Act to make it possible for a city to establish and maintain its own public schools. The other was a letter from Jessop prefacing his own proposals for a common school system for Vancouver Island.[19] His letter stated that these proposals were based on "the admirable school system of Canada West" which with some slight modification would be suitable for Vancouver Island. The report, a synopsis of which was printed under his letter, had as he stated, "been furnished to a member of the nonchalant school committee. This gentleman, however, to do him justice, has frequently urged the necessity of something being done on this important subject. The whole onus, therefore, of the Committee's apathy rests on the shoulders of Mr. Duncan, the chairman, who after repeated solicitations has persistently neglected his duty as enjoined upon him by the House of Assembly."

Jessop then proceeded to outline a five-point plan for a common school system:

FIRSTLY — Common Schools "supported wholly or in part from the public revenue" must be "strictly non-sectarian".

SECONDLY — School trustees should be elected annually by the householders and freeholders in a school district. In country districts there would be three-man boards and in incorporated cities and towns two trustees per ward. He proposed a system of retirement by rotation to insure that a board would always contain some experienced trustees. The school boards, following eastern Canadian practice, should have possession and control of the school property and be responsible for its proper maintenance.

THIRDLY — A "Council of Public Instruction" should be appointed by the Governor. Its duties would include making regulations for "the organization, government and discipline of common schools and for the classification of schools and teachers", the approval of textbooks and the examination and certification of teachers.

FOURTHLY — A Superintendent of Education would be appointed by the Governor. This official who would also be a member of the Council of Public Instruction would be empowered to "apportion annually all moneys granted or provided by the House of Assembly" for school purposes "according to the ratio of population and average school attendance", to visit the schools regularly and to examine and report on all aspects of their condition, the work of the teachers and the progress of the pupils. He would be required annually to report to the Governor on the state of the Colony's schools.

FIFTHLY — Common School teachers would all have to be qualified and have certificates issued them by the Council of Public Instruction. Their duties as outlined followed the commonly accepted traditions of the profession.

The day following the publication of Jessop's proposals for a public school system, the report of the House of Assembly's Committee on Education appeared in the press.[20] There were remarkable similarities between the committee's recommendations and Jessop's proposals. The committee recognized the need for a system of common schools for the colony and that these would have to be supported wholly or in part from the general revenues of the colony and that land be reserved for schools in "the laying out of all villages, towns and districts." Should the government grant be insufficient for the educational purposes of a district, a school rate to raise the extra funds needed should be levied and collected by the Government within that district. "In order to extend the advantages of a Common School education to

44

all persons, any system to be successful should be non-sectarian." The report, in common with Jessop's scheme, recommended elected boards of school trustees for each district, a Council of Public Instruction and a Superintendent of Education, but would have the Council and the Superintendent appointed *annually*. The report ended by recommending that its proposals be "made operative by the immediate introduction and passage of an Act."

In the meantime Victoria's first Mayor, Tom Harris, in response to a petition signed by many citizens, had called a public meeting in the Victoria Theatre. It was held the evening following the publication of the committee's report.[21] About five hundred attended. Mayor Harris, a great massive man, bald and bearded, chaired the meeting. He loved to chair meetings and the more boisterous they were the more he enjoyed himself. When John Cochrane moved that the city have a free common school in a central location, non-sectarian, efficiently conducted and open to all classes in the community, the Rev. Charles T. Woods, supported by the Rev Mr. Cridge, countered with an amendment "that the Bible must be recognized as the foundation of all true knowledge." This opened up a very spirited debate on the definitions of non-sectarianism and on the high cost of sending children to the existing denominational schools. The education committee of the House also came under criticism for its apparent apathy and inaction. When the mayor finally put the question to a vote the original motion carried by a large majority. No doubt remained that the citizens wanted free nonsectarian schools.

Dr. Helmcken, the speaker of the House of Assembly and Amor de Cosmos, the member from Victoria, rose to counter the charge that the Assembly was apathetic toward education. De Cosmos then gave an outline of the entire system proposed by the committee in its Report to the House. A later speaker observed that "he did not think this Report would have yet seen the light unless the cat-'o-nine tails had been exhibited in the shape of public movement". De Cosmos questioned the suitability of Jessop's school building if it were being considered for the new school. He claimed that Jessop on a previous occasion had told him it was too small for this purpose. Jessop denied having said this but only that the playground might be considered too small although, he pointed out, it was very well equipped.

The committee finally decided to write to the Legislature petitioning that body to establish a public school system immediately. A deputation was selected to interview Governor Kennedy and press their case.

It consisted of John J. Cochrane, George Cruickshank, W. M. Scarby, S. Hoffman, J. T. Little, J. E. MacMillan, J. T. Pediwell, C. B. Young and John Jessop.

Two days later this deputation met Governor Kennedy and presented the resolutions passed at the public meeting. Cochrane was the spokesman. "The Legislature", he was quoted as saying, "has appropriated a sum of $5,000 to erect a school house on the District Reserve but the meeting came to the conclusion that it was too far from the city and they therefore called on His Excellency to ask him either to prevent the appropriation or to enable the money to be expended in a different way", or at least to use it to provide temporary accommodations in the centre of the city.[22] When Jessop, at the Governor's request, read the resolutions of the meeting, Kennedy enquired about the location of the school reserve. He concurred with the deputation that it seemed too far from the central part of town and said that he would think it "advisable to rent some place in the city for school purposes."

On the question of a non-sectarian school system Kennedy agreed wholeheartedly with the deputation. "A man may be a very good schoolmaster," he said, "and yet a very indifferent theologian."

The same day the *Colonist* commented editorially on the deputation's reception by the Governor. "He heartily concurs in the non-sectarian resolutions of the meeting, and promises to give every assistance to establish common schools throughout the colony."

In early May the school bill came before the House and was given second reading, The editorial comment of the *Colonist* at that time was approval in principle but with a contrary note not to imperil its passage by making the school system too expensive. The House decided to postpone further action on the bill until the 1865 session.

A few days later many Victoria parents, in a last desperate attempt to keep their schools going, petitioned the Government to appropriate sufficient funds for the schools until legislation should set up a new system. When this came before the House in the form of a motion to grant $2,500 for school purposes only the three Victoria members supported it. Jessop's friend, Leonard McClure, who was now the editor of the *Colonist*,[23] explained the opposition: "The city members were arrayed on the one side and the country members on the other— or in other words the representatives of five sixths of the population were in favor of giving the children of the poorer classes in Victoria facilities for obtaining an education while the other sixth — the

Victoria in 1862 showing the old James Bay Bridge leading into Government Street. From Mayne's Four Years in British Columbia and Vancouver Island, 1862. B.C. Archives.

Craigflower School, Victoria. A Colonial School. B.C. Archives.

Cache Creek Boarding School. B.C. Archives.

Bird's eye view of Victoria in 1878. B.C. Archives.

representatives of logs and stumps — voted against it and of course defeated the project."[24]

It was a year before the Legislature considered again the question of a school system. During that year what Jessop did, where he lived and how he was employed is not known. His school was closed but while the building had been advertised for sale he did not sell it. It is very probable that he may have turned again to the newspaper business and that McClure may have employed him at the *Colonist*.

FOOTNOTES

[1] B.C. Archives, M.S. F395.

[2] *Colonist*, September 14, 1859.

[3] *Colonist*, January 10, 1863, p. 3.

[4] Kerr, J. B., *op. cit.*, p. 207.

[5] Douglas to Archibald Barclay, May 16, 1850, B.C. Archives.

[6] Ontario Archives. This letter is quoted in Spragge, George W., "An Early Letter from Victoria, V.I.", *Canadian Historical Review,* Toronto, University of Toronto Press, 1948, Vol. 29, pp. 54-56.

[7] *Colonist*, January 10, 1863, p. 3.

[8] *Colonist*, December 24, 1861, p. 3.

[9] Kerr, J. B. *op. cit.*, p. 207.

[10] *Colonist*, December 24, 1862, p. 3.

[11] *Ibid.,* August 11, 1862, p. 3.

[12] *Ibid.,* December 24, 1862, p. 3.

[13] *loc. cit.,* p. 3.

[14] *Colonist*, January 10, 1863, p. 3.

[15] Johnson, F. H., *A History of Public Education in British Columbia,* Vancouver, University of British Columbia Publications Centre, 1964, p. 30.

[16] *Ibid.,* p. 30.

[17] *Colonist*, March 22, 1864, p. 3.

[18] *Ibid.,* April, 1864, p. 3.

[19] *Ibid.,* April 8, 1864.

[20] *Ibid.,* April 9, 1864, p. 3.

[21] *Ibid.,* April 11, 1864, p. 3.

[22] *Ibid.,* April 13, 1864, p. 3.

[23] McClure took over the *British Colonist* from de Cosmos in October, 1863 and continued as editor until June, 1866.

[24] *Colonist*, June 9, 1864, p. 2.

CHAPTER FIVE

Free Schools, But Not For Long

In May 1865 the Vancouver Island Legislature acceded to the popular demand for free non-sectarian schools by passing *An Act Respecting Common Schools*. It was, in its way, an historic step in Canadian history. In the same year Nova Scotia also passed an act similarly guaranteeing free non-sectarian schooling. Only one other colony of the British North American possessions had preceded Vancouver Island in establishing these elements of a democratic society, Prince Edward Island, the sister colony on the Atlantic Seaboard.[1] Not until a half-century later did the Mother Country provide free elementary education for all of her own children.

In the early stages of the bill it was touch and go as to whether or not to grant free schooling. The Legislative Council wanted to charge a small fee of fifty cents a month but Leonard McClure, now representing Victoria, condemned this as destroying, for mere penny-pinching economy, the important principle of free education — and the Assembly deleted the fee clause.[2] The Act in its final form, however, did not specifically promise that schools should be free but Section XV guaranteed that, "Every Common School shall be open to the Children of Persons of all Denominations" and made no mention of fees. The *Colonist* observed, "We are not disposed to cavil at the imperfections of the bill so long as the two great principles — free schools and a non-sectarian system of education are enunciated."[3]

The act was very concise, containing sixteen brief sections. It established a General Board of Education of no fewer than nine persons appointed by the Governor. All school property was vested in this General Board. The Governor was authorized to appoint a superintendent of Education (at a salary of $1,500 per annum) whose term of office would be for one year and who would be ex officio secretary of the General Board. He was empowered to inspect the schools and report thereon to the Board. This Board was to exercise full control over curricula, textbooks and the duties of teachers but all teachers would be appointed directly by the Governor. The Governor could "if he shall think it expedient to do so" appoint a local board of education which would have a function purely advisory to the General Board. Section XIII stated: "All schools established under the Provisions of this Act shall be conducted strictly upon Non-Sectarian Principles. Books inculcating the highest Morality shall be selected for the use of such Schools, and all Books of a Religious Character, teaching Denominational Dogmas shall be strictly excluded therefrom." It would be lawful, however, for clergy of every denomination "at stated intervals to be fixed by the General Board of Education" to visit the schools and give religious education in a separate room to children of their particular persuasion.

Kennedy appointed to the General Board of Education Dr. William Fraser Tolmie, a Scottish physician and an old Hudson's Bay official, Dr. I. W. Powell, a Canadian physician and friend of Sir John A. Macdonald, Joseph Despard Pemberton, the Colonial surveyor who had laid out the city of Victoria, William John McDonald (one of the first settlers in the colony and later to be elevated to the Canadian Senate), Thomas Trounce, I. Wright, D. M. Lang, John J. Cochrane and C. Graham Alston. Tolmie was elected the first chairman. This was the board which until 1869 was to administer all the schools of Vancouver Island. There was no local school board for the city of Victoria. First item on the Board's agenda was the appointment of a Superintendent of Education. Jessop was one who applied for the position but the man the Board chose was Alfred Waddington, a British-born Victoria merchant and a much more prominent person in the colony. He was very much in the public eye at the time for having promoted a wagon road from the head of Bute Inlet to the Cariboo. The previous year the Chilcotin Indians had risen in rebellion against this intrusion into their territory, had killed nineteen of his workmen and had put an end to the project. In later years Jessop confided to Premier John Foster McCreight that he would have received this appointment at the time "but for the heavy misfortunes of the late Mr. Waddington which enlisted a strong sympathy in his behalf."[4]

The Board with its new Superintendent next proceeded to deal with the matter of the Central School. In June they decided to rent the premises from Jessop for sixty dollars a month and to appoint him principal at a salary of $1,200 per annum. The school was to be divided into a boys' and a girls' department and Mrs. Elizabeth Fisher was appointed to teach the girls at a monthly salary of sixty dollars.

The content of a school curriculum in those days depended largely on the choice of textbooks. It is rather interesting to note that the Board decided to adopt "those selected and used by the Council of Public Instruction in Upper Canada."[5] Jessop had introduced this series to Victoria when he had first opened his Central School. It had originally been prepared for the National schools of Ireland. Ryerson had seen the books in use there and had introduced them to Upper Canada. More than one generation of Canadians (and Irishmen) learned to read from the little green covered Irish National Readers.

Newly painted and whitewashed, the Central School on Fort Street opened its doors to boys and girls on August 1. The opening was a gala event to celebrate the inauguration under the auspices of the Board of Education, of the opening of the first Free School. The school was filled to capacity on that occasion not only by 117 lively boys and 91 excitable girls but by all the official visitors including Governor Kennedy, Anglican Bishop Hills, Mayor Harris, Superintendent Waddington, the clergy and the members of the Board of Education.

It was soon evident that extra accommodation would be needed and the Board arranged for the rental of the nearby Congregational Church on Fort Street. The school was then split into a Girls' Central, which remained in the original building, and a Boys' Central which removed to the Congregational Church with Jessop.

The Free School system was off to a good start. There was keen interest on the part of the Board and Superintendent and there seemed to be great popular support from the citizens.

One of Waddington's essential duties was to inspect the schools and to report on what he saw. This he did far more frequently than inspectors today with many more teachers in their districts are able to do. From his reports[6] we can form some picture of Jessop as a schoolmaster although merit, like beauty, is in the eye of the observer, and the observer in this case does not seem to have been a great admirer of Jessop nor was he an experienced teacher. When he first visited the school before it moved into the Congregational Church he found Jessop coping frantically with 117 pupils aided by a monitor. Waddington noted: "Lesson Geography, answers middling, many of the children new scholars. Upper class on geography and the terrestrial globe. Answers satisfactory and intelligent. Lesson of music: Noisy and occasionally out of tune; room for great improvement." Of a later visit he wrote, "Class in Algebra composed of 6 scholars. Examination in Compound division. Result tolerable." To have brought a huge class of these wild young pioneer lads to the point where he could teach them anything in mathematics in such a short time would seem to have merited some accolade a little warmer than "tolerable".

Jessop's first public examination under the Free School Act took place on July 3, 1866 before a large audience consisting of Mayor Harris, members of the Board of Education, the clergy, some teachers and many parents, particularly the ladies. After "a short allocution" by the Superintendent three of the city clergymen conducted examinations—Dr. Evans in Geography, History, Philosophy and Mechanics, the Reverend Mr. Garrett in Geometry and Algebra, and the Reverend Mr. Somerville in Grammar. Waddington considered the reading was "fair" to "middling", the arithmetic of Jessop's senior class (vulgar fractions and decimals) was very poor and the grammar of the same class "still worse", although this class somewhat redeemed its laurels in Geography and History ("remarkably good"), Philosophy ("very good") and Writing ("a great general improvement"). The singing of the whole school was "very fair". In conclusion, "short allocutions" were made by the Superintendent, by Mr. Jessop, Dr. Evans, Mr. Garrett and Mr. Somerville, after which "the names of the Boys most deserving for progress and good behaviour were called over."[7]

On a later occasion Waddington visited the Central School (Boys) at 9:00 a.m. and returned the monthly written examinations. "Number of scholars on the register 55. Since August last 51 pupils have left the Island! Heard the fourth reader class, subject William Tell, a difficult one to read well. Expression middling. The children neat, clean and orderly."[8]

The central location of Jessop's school on Fort Street had been one of the main reasons for its existence. Even when it was first erected it was in the center of the business district but Jessop had provided a fenced-in play area with gymnastic equipment to keep the children off the street at recesses. However, with the move of the boys up the street to the nearby Congregational Church which lacked any suitable play area, there were frequent complaints from shopkeepers and neighbors about the rambunctious behavior of the lads. The Mayor had written the Board complaining of the lack of playgrounds for them, thus forcing them to play on the street "to the great annoyance of the neighbors and foot passengers." Waddington's journal records similar complaints of boys playing in the streets "and

52

more particularly on the sidewalks when coming out of school, which means in fact almost all day on account of the frequent recesses." On another occasion, "Visited the Central School, boys, at 9:00 a.m. on account of a complaint from Mrs. Moss that the boys climb on her roof, throw stones into the yard and are very impertinent." Boys in that Victorian age were expected by adults to be polite, respectful and obedient, but they were no more lacking than modern children in primitive animal spirits. Confinement in stuffy, packed school rooms, sitting for hours on uncomfortable and often backless seats must have required a release of energy when they emerged from their prisons comparable to the explosion of a hydrogen bomb.

The Board of Education in 1865 had decreed that the schools would have six weeks holidays in the year — two weeks at Christmas and New Year and four weeks in midsummer, "the Midsummer vacation to be made to coincide as far as possible with the harvest in the Country Districts and with the reopening of the private schools after the vacation in the towns."[9]

In the meantime financial problems had developed in both the colonies which were to cripple the Free School system of Vancouver Island. The flow of gold from the Cariboo mines on which the economies of both colonies had been so dependent began to decrease as early as 1863 and by 1866 had reached a perilous low. British Columbia's wealth was a direct reflection of mining activity. Vancouver Island's prosperity depended upon Victoria's position as a port of entry and distributing center for both colonies so that the economics of both were as vitally interrelated as the health of Siamese twins.

Politically British Columbia had been created a separate Crown Colony but, until Douglas retired, with the same Governor as Vancouver Island. The latter colony, however, possessed a more advanced political system with its House of Assembly, whereas British Columbia had no representative government until, after much agitation, Douglas set up a Legislative Council just before his retirement in 1864. At the same time as Governor Kennedy replaced Douglas in Vancouver Island, Frederick Seymour was sent out as Governor of British Columbia. Finally, the Imperial Government decided that the mining and trade recession in the two colonies could best be combatted by uniting them under the British Columbia Act which came into effect by proclamation on November 19, 1866. It was a shotgun marriage, welcomed at the time by few on either side of the strait. When the men-o'-war in Victoria's harbor fired a salute to the new united colony, Sir James Douglas from the sidelines commented, "A funeral procession with minute guns would have been more appropriate."[10]

Vancouver Island was absorbed into the political constitution of British Columbia, thereby losing its elective assembly and coming under the authority of Governor Seymour and his Legislative Council which was increased to provide Island representation. Kennedy was recalled (not unwillingly). Victoria ceased to be a free port but it was finally selected as the capital, much to the consternation of the citizens of New Westminster.

For those interested in Vancouver Island's free school system the union represented a setback as British Columbia had no school system and had taken no legislative action in this regard. Douglas, when Governor, had given a grant of £100 to assist a non-sectarian school which the Reverend Robert Jamieson and a committee of New Westminster citizens had organized, but this school like other private schools, charged fees.[11]

What would now be the fate of the Board of Education and the Island's Free Schools? The British Columbia Act did state that, until legislation provided otherwise, the laws in force in Vancouver Island before the union would continue in force and effect.[12] On this basis the Board of Education tried to carry on with the administration of the Vancouver Island Schools. But it was not left long in doubt as to Governor Seymour's attitude toward the Island's free schools. He strongly favored a non-sectarian system. As he told his new Legislative Council, "The Government has not undertaken to prove to the Jew that the Messiah has indeed arrived, to rob the Roman Catholic of his belief in the merciful intercession of the Blessed Virgin, to give special support to the Church of England, to mitigate the acidity of the Calvinist doctrines of some believers, or to determine authoritatively the number of Sacraments."[13] However much he might concur in the non-sectarian aspect of the Island system he did not, however, agree that the state should provide free schooling. Britain had not done this. "Every man who respects himself," he told his Council, "would not desire to have his children instructed without some pecuniary sacrifice on his own part. The state may aid the parent, but ought not to relieve him of his own responsibility".

Even before the union of the colonies the Island system had been in financial trouble. Governor Kennedy could not see how, with

Vancouver Island's reduced revenues, it would be possible to continue to pay for free schools. On August 31, 1866 he had notified the General Board that he "could not guarantee payment of any further Expenditure either of salaries or rents" beyond that date. The Board had communicated this bitter news to the teachers without terminating their appointments. Jessop and two other teachers stated their intention nevertheless "to continue their functions for the present at least without insisting upon any further guarantee".[14]

When Seymour took over as Governor he notified the Board of Education in December 1866 that "the whole system of public schools required reforming."[15] This was understandable in the light of the union of the two colonies but nothing was done in this regard for three years. In June 1867 the Colonial Secretary informed the Board that the Government's total budget for education in British Columbia was $10,000 and that he was devoting $6,000 of this sum to the Vancouver Island Board, adding that he "will leave it to the Board to determine how the public interests in the matter can be best served, but the amount now offered must besides promoting the current education of the children, serve to extinguish any liabilities of the Government for past services."[16] When the Board protested that this would not begin to cover their indebtedness which by that time was about $11,000, Seymour simply reminded the Board that Vancouver Island had been apportioned $6,000 out of the $10,000 granted by the Legislature for Education purposes and "should the greater self-reliance of the Mainland leave a surplus in the grant, His Excellency will be happy to hand it over to you but he would urge that you make your arrangements irrespective of this consideration."[17] The Board then paid a first instalment on the salary arrears up to December 1866, the first money it had disbursed to its teachers since August 1866.

Jessop in the meantime was carrying on as best he could in the midst of this controversy, and in common with the other teachers, feeling more and more the pinch of penury. He was coping as best he could with the inconveniences of teaching a large class of about sixty boys in a church without adequate facilities. When a high wind in May 1867 blew the steeple askew, the authorities propped it into a vertical stance again with stout timbers — the British Columbian equivalent of the flying buttress. The next month the Board informed Jessop and two other teachers, Burr and Bryant, that while retaining their services they would have to reduce their salaries to $75 a month. They decided also to let out the female assistant at the Girls' Central

School and abandon the Congregational Church, placing both boys and girls in the Central School building and limiting attendance there to children under ten years of age. Jessop accepted the salary of $75 a month, a further reduction to $30 a month in the rent for his building and he agreed to pay for the janitorial work himself. He did, however, object strenuously to the Board restricting attendance at his school to children under age ten "thus reducing it to an infant school without the possibility of monitorial aid, besides separating children of the same family, interfering with the preferences of the parents and other serious inconveniences."[18]

Had Jessop some assurance that even his reduced rent and salary would be regularly paid he would have been content to continue on this basis in order that the Free School policy might endure. But he knew that there was little hope of this. Therefore in July 1867 he told the Board that, in view of the financial difficulties, he would be prepared to carry on his school under its supervision but proposed that he be permitted to charge a fee of one dollar per child per month. With the aid of an appropriation from the Board of $300 he offered to carry on his school and pay all expenses of rent, fuel, etc.[19]

This, of course, would mean the end of the Free School principle and the Board was not yet prepared to capitulate on this point. They appealed to the governor to save the schools by imposing a special tax for their support and when this brought no response they finally called a public meeting in Victoria to put their case before the citizens.

On August 12 the weather was warm and the meeting warmer. It was held in the Congregational Church which was crammed to capacity. Mayor Macdonald, acting as chairman, explained that the purpose of the meeting was to ask the opinion of the public as to "what course should be followed in the present financial embarrassments of the Colony to maintain the present system of education."[20] Dr. Powell, now chairman of the Board of Education, explained that the Board were "in favor of continuing the Free system but were unable to open the schools owing to the want of funds." He then read to the audience a long report which gave a history of the Board's difficulties from the very beginning under Governor Kennedy up to the present crisis and the latest unsympathetic reply from Governor Seymour. He concluded by saying that "if no more funds were forthcoming the schools must remain closed."

The Board's proposal that the Legislature impose a special school tax was debated and opposed by Dr. Helmcken and by supporters of

56

some of the religious schools. Jessop addressed the crowd and announced that his school would reopen on Monday morning and "he would trust as he had trusted before, to the Government and Colony to defray his expenses (applause)."

The meeting ended by adopting a resolution "respectfully requesting that His Excellency the Governor be pleased to place the additional sum of $2,000 to which this meeting considers the people of Vancouver Island fairly entitled, at the disposal of the Board."

Jessop reopened his school in August 1867 "under his own responsibility and pending the decision of the Board" with a full house of 92 children, 40 of whom were girls. All the school property had been removed from the Congregational Church and those premises had been vacated.[21]

In September the Board received a final polite "No" from Seymour to their request for financial assistance. Waddington then resigned and Jessop offered to perform the duties of the Superintendent for the remainder of the year if an assistant teacher could be appointed to the Central School. Even in such a discouraging situation Jessop sought authority and the opportunity to show what he could do for education. The Board made no move to fill the vacancy.

By December the Board had informed the Governor again of the "almost destitute condition of the Teachers." Jessop had sought and been granted permission to hold an Evening School for adults in the Central School House. This he hoped would gather in a few dollars in fees. Once more the Board had to notify its teachers that they could expect no more salary and that the schools would not reopen after Christmas.

To the teachers this Christmas promised little of the traditional mirth and good cheer. But just at the darkest hour they received a little encouragement and much needed funds thanks to the philanthropy of an American travelling circus proprietor, Mr. G. Bartholomew, who staged a "Benefit Concert" in aid of the Free Schools.[22] The barbaric splendor of the old Theatre Royal was packed to its rafters for the occasion by enthusiastic Victorians who roared their approval of the two clowns, "Monsieurs LeClerq and Garneau and their droll habits", were suitably awed by the "grand Chinese entree" and loudly applauded the efforts of the Victoria Amateur Dramatic Club. "The vast audience remained until the close," reported the *Colonist*, "and at the fall of the curtain dispersed with cheers." The concert realized $434 which the Board divided among the teachers.

Jessop must have made out a little better the next year. Perhaps he could now earn a comfortable living from the fees of his day and evening pupils. Perhaps he had other sources of income of which we have no record. Perhaps he subscribed to the faith that two can live more cheaply than one. In any case he decided to marry.

The "object of his affections" was a young schoolmistress, Margaret (also called Meta) Faucette. Born in Ireland, where her father was a prominent Dublin physician, she had come out to the West Coast of America in 1862 and had taught across the water in Washington Territory in the village of Coupeville on Whidby Island.[23] She had moved to Victoria and in 1863 had opened a private school for girls. An advertisement appearing in the *Colonist* of July 1864 proclaimed that "Miss Faucette's Academy for Young Ladies will re-open on Monday 25th Instant . . . Having Enlarged Her School-Room and engaged the services of an Assistant, Miss Faucette is prepared to receive an additional number of pupils . . . The course of instruction comprises all the branches of a Thorough English Education, viz. Reading, Writing, Arithmetic, French, Spanish, Singing in Class, Plain and Ornamental Needlework. Terms $3 to $5 per month according to age and advancement. Extras — music and drawing."[24] She had applied, unsuccessfully, in 1865 for the position of teacher in the Central Girls' School and had submitted letters of reference from Dr. James Dickson of Victoria who testified to her "high character, good education, ability as a teacher, sound judgement and moral worth". The Reverend Edward Cridge had apparently examined her school and had approved of "the progress of the pupils and general order at her school on Douglas Street and her good mode of instruction"[25] She was an Anglican, Jessop an active Methodist, a trustee of his church and Superintendent of the Sunday School.[26] Nothing more is known of her. Whether she was plain or pretty, who knows? No picture of her has survived. They were married in Victoria on March 30, 1868 by the Rev. A. Browning, a Methodist minister.[27] After their marriage the young bride continued to teach in her "Academy for Young Ladies."

After Waddington's resignation the Board of Education held few meetings. In April it threatened to resign. This brought some response from the Council which passed a resolution to pay off the indebtedness to the schools. In June the Board received the sum of $2,000, half of which it used to pay off arrears dating back to December 15, 1866 and the other half for expenses incurred in the current year 1868. In

March 1869 the Board held its final meeting and resigned. There was no role for it to play under the new school legislation which the Council passed.

This was known as the Common School Ordinance of 1869 and was the first and only school legislation to apply to the united colony of British Columbia.[28] It repealed the Island's Free School Act and placed all authority for the schools of British Columbia under the Governor in Council which body could create school districts, apportion the school grants, appoint and remove the teachers, decide on textbooks and make any rules or regulations for the management and governance of common schools. While it could "provide for the establishment and election of local boards" it retained under its own charge all school lands and properties. The school grant was not to exceed $500 per annum per teacher. The non-sectarian principle was retained in the section which specified that textbooks must be "of a proper and non-sectarian character."

Obviously the $500 grant per teacher would not go far toward covering the costs of education. It was clearly the intention of the Act to shift a large part of the financial responsibility for the schools to the municipal councils. They in turn were to initiate by-laws which would ask the citizens to approve a poll tax of two dollars per annum for each male resident in a district. Two dollars would seem a modest enough contribution but the legislators did not take into account the peculiar reluctance of citizens in that age of laissez-faire to pay local taxes.

Under the new order Jessop was retained as principal by the Victoria city council and his school reopened in August 1869 to a cheerful note of optimism heralded by the *Colonist*. "The Council have decided to make the schools as free as air and to provide the ways and means necessary to their maintenance, beyond the $500 allowed by the Colonial Government, a poll tax will be levied. Let it fall on all male adults and not exclusively on householders. If all of them have not children it is their lookout and not their country's."[29]

Judging by the glacial speed with which the local authorities in Victoria carried out their commitment, they might well have been waiting for a new generation of taxpayers to grow up. Four months after the act was passed the Victoria school district was defined and a local school board elected. Another three months passed before the board proceeded to pass a tax by-law and another month for it to secure the approval of the new Governor, Anthony Musgrave. The board then learned that a public meeting must be held to approve the by-law. This took another month and a month more for the Governor to approve this. It was late February 1870 before the collection of the tax began and by June the board had collected only $516.[30]

Up to the end of 1869 Jessop and the other Victoria teachers had received nothing more than their $500 Government grants. In May 1870 the Colonial Secretary informed the Victoria board that the grant for the year 1870 would be paid only on satisfactory evidence that it was being matched by Victoria. The board could not give such assurance and consequently the teachers received nothing. Most adult males were ignoring the tax and the board refused to prosecute them.

In October of 1869 Jessop, on behalf of the Victoria teachers, had presented a petition to Governor Musgrave recounting the shameful story of their treatment and listing in detail the arrears in salaries and rents which amounted in total to $3918. Musgrave replied that there was no fund provided by the Legislature from which he could liquidate such a claim and he refused to accept responsibility for debts incurred before his incumbency.[31] Another letter from Jessop to the Governor in April 1870 received a curt reply that he could not say when their arrears would be paid.[32] And that was that!

In the same month the Council had passed an amendment to the Common School Ordinance which authorized the appointment of an inspector or inspectors. Jessop lost no time in applying to Governor Musgrave for this position. His motives, as he stated them in his letter of application, were interesting.[33] "Being fully aware that no pecuniary consideration will be attached to the office, I am only activated by a desire to do what I can in securing some uniformity in the system of teaching in the schools over which the Victoria inspector may have supervision. So far nothing has been done in this direction since the Public School System was first brought into operation. Each teacher has a method of his or her own, which is carried out with no regard whatever to assimilation with other schools. This has always been a drawback on their general efficiency which a practical Inspector could, to a very great degree, remove by visiting the schools; explaining his own system to the teachers and observing theirs; by inaugurating and encouraging Teachers' Meetings at stated intervals for the purpose of discussing and explaining the systems made use of by each; adopting such methods as may be approved of, and thus gradually attaining some degree of uniformity." Musgrave's instructions to his secretary were to "return Mr. Jessop's certificates and inform him civilly, that his services are declined." The Governor appointed as "Inspector-General" E. Graham Alston who had been a member of the former General Board of Education of Vancouver Island.

Jessop and the Victoria teachers carried on with their thankless task until the summer with no improvement in the situation and no further salary payments — the victims of a governmental system where both the central and local authorities callously disregarded the plight of the penniless teachers and shirked their responsibilities to the children. Finally on September 13, 1870, the *Colonist* carried this message to the public of Victoria over the signatures of John Jessop and W. H. Burr:

> WE THE TEACHERS OF THE PUBLIC SCHOOL for Victoria City and District, finding it impossible to continue teaching, in consequence of non payment of the monies due to us for our services, are reluctantly obliged to close the school till such time as proper provision shall be made for punctual payment of our salaries.
>
> Eighteen months have elapsed since the new School Ordinance became law, during which time we have only received from all sources six months' pay. We deem this explanation necessary under the circumstances; and believe that a discriminating public will not censure us for taking a step which is unavoidable.[34]

It was the first teachers' strike in Canadian history and the longest in duration. Alston was entirely sympathetic. "I think the teachers should have taken this step months ago."[35] The *Colonist* condemned the Government and added with grim irony, "The Public Schools being closed, children appear upon the streets in considerable force, but it must not be supposed that education is at a standstill. Not by any means; and if some of these youngsters do not soon become worthy graduates of the School of Vice, it will not be for want of an opportunity. There is talk of the Government assuming the responsibilities of paying the teachers; but we fear it will end in 'talk' ".[36]

Jessop was obliged to return once more "to the Printing Office", as he said, "to obtain the necessaries of life."[37] His wife in the meantime had been operating her private school, the "Roseville Academy" for young ladies, and perhaps had provided the mainstay of their existence in these lean years.[38]

The schools of Victoria remained closed for two years until the man who had led the strike was himself in a position of authority to solve the problem.

FOOTNOTES

[1] P.E.I. established free schools in 1852.

[2] *Colonist,* April 13, 1865.

[3] *Ibid.,* May 13, 1865.

[4] Jessop to J. F. McCreight, 26 March, 1872, B.C. Archives.

[5] Proceedings of the Board of Education of Vancouver Island, July 11, 1865. B.C. Archives. This is the principal source of information on the schools from 1865 to 1867.

[6] Journal of Alfred Waddington, 1865-1867, B.C. Archives.

[7] *Ibid.,* July 3, 1866.

[8] *Ibid.,* June 10, 1867.

[9] Proceedings of the Board of Education of Vancouver Island. Dec. 7, 1865, B.C. Archives.

[10] Diary of Martha Douglas Harris, entry of Nov. 19, 1866, B.C. Archives.

[11] See Johnson, F. Henry, *A History of Public Education in British Columbia,* Vancouver, U.B.C. Publications Centre, 1964, p. 23.

[12] An Act for the Union of the Colony of Vancouver Island with the Colony of British Columbia, 1886, section 5.

[13] Journals of the Legislative Council of British Columbia, 1867, B.C. Archives, 29, 30.

[14] Waddington's Journal, Sept. 1, 1866, B.C. Archives.

[15] Proceedings of the Board of Education of Vancouver Island, Dec. 28, 1866, B.C. Archives.

[16] *Ibid.,* p. 114.

[17] *Ibid.,* p. 104.

[18] *Ibid.,* July 1, 1867.

[19] Correspondence, Board of Education of Vancouver Is. p. 75, B.C. Archives.

[20] *Colonist,* August 12, 1867, p. 3.

[21] Proceedings, Board of Education, August 20, 1867.

[22] *Colonist,* December 18, 1867, p. 3.

[23] Waddington's Journal, B.C. Archives, June 13, 1867. Her documents were being returned by Waddington, also Kerr, *op. cit.,* pp. 208, 209.

[24] *Colonist,* July 19, 1864, p. 4.

[25] Waddington's Journal, B.C. Archives, June 13, 1867.

[26] *Methodist Recorder,* Victoria, February 1900, p. 9.

[27] *Colonist,* March 31, 1868, p. 3.

[28] British Columbia Statutes. Common School Ordinance No. 21, B.C. Archives. See also Johnson, *Op. cit.,* pp. 37, 38. There was an amendment passed in 1870 providing for the appointment of inspectors of schools.

[29] *Colonist,* August 3, 1869, p. 3.

[30] Alston to Haskin (Colonial Secretary), July 14, 1870, B.C. Archives.

[31] Hankin to Jessop, October 18, 1869, B.C. Archives.

[32] Jessop to Hankin and reply, April 8, 1870, B.C. Archives.

[33] Jessop to Musgrave, April 25, 1870, B.C. Archives.

[34] *Colonist,* September 13, 1870.

[35] Alston to Hankin, September 14, 1870, B.C. Archives.

[36] *Colonist,* September 14, 1870.

[37] Jessop to J. F. McCreight, March 26, 1872, B.C. Archives.

[38] *Colonist,* July 31, 1869, p. 3.

CHAPTER SIX

Confederation And The Hustings

The Free School issue had arisen at a time when the attention of the colony's political leaders, and of the general public, was focussed on a development of much broader scope and much greater concern and this in itself may have accounted for some of the apathy toward public education which had been so discouraging to Jessop and his colleagues. Ever since the union of the two Pacific colonies there had been an atmosphere of growing unrest in British Columbia. This was due to the combination of an economic recession with an unsatisfactory constitution which had given the colonists only a limited representative government and none of the features of responsible government to which Canadians and British were accustomed.[1]

Moreover, two international developments of 1867 had raised in the minds of many the question of the future political affiliation of the colony. On March 30, 1867, Secretary of State Seward arranged for the United States' purchase of Alaska from Russia for $7,200,000. Three months later the Dominion of Canada was formed from a four-province confederation of British North American colonies. The future seemed to offer the colony three alternatives — (1) to retain the status quo as a Crown Colony of Great Britain. (This had the support of the small official group led by such men as Governor Seymour, Philip Hankin the Colonial Secretary and Dr. Helmcken.) (2) To seek annexation by the United States. Since the majority of the colonists were Americans there would seem to be strong support for this stand although an annexation petition circulated in Victoria in 1869 contained only 104 names.[2] (3) To seek confederation with Canada. The main support for this alternative was in the small but vocal Canadian minority led by such activists as Robson and de Cosmos. When the young Dominion lost no time in acquiring the vast Hudson's Bay Company domains and converting these into its

North West Territories Canada no longer seemed so distant a country since its territories now extended to British Columbia's Rocky Mountain frontier. Finally, the creation out of these Federal territories of Canada's fifth province of Manitoba in 1870 transformed the idea of confederation from what many had considered a political pipe dream into a very plausible proposition.

What could confederation with Canada offer which might make this option the more attractive one to British Columbians? It was commonly suggested from the "Birdcages" to the pool halls of Victoria that confederation would bring prosperity. Canadian money, it was rumored, might finance many needed projects such as a drydock at Esquimalt. Amor de Cosmos proposed that a wagon road to Ontario be an essential term of union and when the Canadian Government offered to go him one better and construct a railroad to the Pacific this was the card that turned the trick. The other trump was responsible government. Confederation with Canada would bring a system of responsible government. "What they all try to hold out for here" wrote Philip Hankin to the Duke of Buckingham, "is Responsible Government, and that they are not fit for. Some of them hope by that means to get into Office."[3] As a colony British Columbia had no cabinet, no premier and no party system. Its premiers had been its governors; its cabinets, the colonial officials.

To advance the cause of union, Amor de Cosmos, James Trimble, Robert Beaven and others formed the Confederation League. It held a convention at Yale in September 1868 which adopted resolutions supporting both confederation and responsible government, but two months later the elections for the Legislative Council fought largely on these twin issues showed a decided split between Island and Mainland. The Islanders elected four anti-confederationists (defeating de Cosmos) and the Mainlanders five supporters of confederation. The year 1869 saw three events transpire each of which eased the way toward confederation. Governor Seymour, the champion of the status quo, died suddenly after a brief illness and was replaced as governor by Anthony Musgrave, who in his former gubernatorial post in Newfoundland, had done his best to try to bring that reluctant colony into confederation. This same year the Canadian Government took over the prairies as its North West Territories. Finally, in a by-election de Cosmos regained his seat in the Legislative Council and was now in a better position to carry on his fight for confederation.

In the year 1870, therefore, events in the drama were moving rapidly to a conclusion. In the spring session the Legislature debated the questions of responsible government and confederation and in August sent a three-man delegation, consisting of Dr. Helmcken, Joseph W. Trutch and Dr. R. W. W. Carroll of the Cariboo, to Ottawa to discuss, and if possible arrange, the conditions of union. Ottawa's terms were announced in August. The promise to build a transcontinental railway to the Pacific coast created great enthusiasm among the Confederationists and the public in general.

Governor Musgrave now ordered, by proclamation of the Imperial Government, a change in the constitution of the Legislative Council which would give elected members a majority (nine to be elected and six nominated by the Governor). A writ was accordingly issued for an election in the fall for what Musgrave called his "Transitional Council". This body would have special powers to alter its own constitution and to take the history-making step of ratifying the terms of union with Canada.[4]

The *Colonist* of September 30, 1870 carried the following brief announcement under the heading "The Kootenay District". There is little doubt that the article was written by the new editor John Robson:

There is a very general impression that the gentleman who represented the Kootenay District in the last session of the Legislative Council has no intention of presenting himself for reelection. Be that as it may, there is another Richmond in the field in the person of Mr. John Jessop, well and favorably known in the community. Mr. Jessop is a gentleman in the prime of life, possessing good physical, mental and moral development with considerable experimental knowledge of colonial politics and quite familiar with the history and wants of this colony. He formed one of a small party of hardy and adventurous Canadians who in 1859 crossed the continent through British territory arriving in the colony in January 1860. While the energy and pluck needed for such a trip would appear to indicate the possession of the right kind of stuff for a pioneer colonist, the experiences thereby acquired would not be altogether valueless in legislating upon questions closely associated with the interests of the vast territory which he traversed, and respecting which a very interesting and well-written account from his pen was published in Canada. In politics Mr. Jessop is decidedly liberal and will support the immediate acceptance of the Canadian Tariff of Customs, the inauguration of Responsible Government simultaneously with union and the adoption of a most liberal and comprehensive Education system. Knowing Mr. Jessop as the writer has, ever since he arrived in this colony, we have no hesitation in saying that we think the people of Kootenay would find in him an able and faithful representative, one who would be a valuable addition to the corps of public men. We understand that Mr. Jessop will start for Kootenay this morning and personally visit every part of the District.[5]

Probably no politician ever made such a long and arduous journey to appeal to so small an electorate. The Kootenay constituency included the whole of the Columbia Valley from the Big Bend to the United States border. Yet in this great triangle of lonely mountains and beautiful valleys there were only two small pockets of population — French Creek in the Big Bend and Wild Horse Creek in the southeast. These were both gold mining areas which had had their brief moments of glory a few years before and were destined to join the many ghost towns of the west. The whole riding could muster scarcely seventy-five eligible voters.

Jessop left Victoria on the paddle steamer *Enterprise* to the encouraging farewells of his young wife and friends. At New Westminster he transferred to a river boat which churned its way up the narrowing valley to the head of navigation at the little canyon town of Yale. Here he tossed his saddlebags on to the stage coach and was off on his first trip up the Cariboo Road, that spectacular cliff-hugging creation of the Royal Engineers. "Words", he said, could not express "the grandly sublime scenery . . . the diversified and magnificent views of nature" that surrounded the traveller as he followed this road, climbing, dipping and twisting through the great canyons of the Fraser and Thompson. At Cache Creek he left the stage and hiring a horse, headed east toward Kamloops and the Big Bend. The Hudson's Bay steamboat *Marten*, which during the Big Bend rush of '66 had shuttled the gold seekers and their supplies from Savona's Ferry at the western end of Kamloops Lake to Seymour at the head of Shuswap Lake, had been beached at Kamloops for lack of business.[6] A Government road, however, had been completed only a year before from Savona to Kamloops.[7] From here on he rode the trail along the South Thompson to the wooded shores of the lovely Shuswap Lake, then over the hills to the head of Seymour Arm. Riding in the delightful days of October through the open country of the Thompson, breathing that exhilarating upland air scented with sagebrush, surrounded everywhere by magnificent vistas of lake and stream, of great brown hills capped with dark pines and splotches of golden aspens must have been for Jessop a blessed relaxation after his miserable experiences of the past three years.

From the already abandoned town of Seymour, Jessop set off on the Government trail heading north and east high up over the Gold Range to reach the Columbia, where it was joined by its tributary, the Goldstream. The trail followed this stream to the mining settlements of McCulloch's Creek and French Creek. The former he described as "a melancholy instance of mining decadence. About 14 substantial buildings, some of them with furniture scattered about the floor, reminds the traveller of former prosperous mining operations. Thus far the forest fires have spared them, but in all probability, before many summers pass over, this once flourishing town will be among the things that were."[8]

Four miles farther on he found the other mining camp in a less depressing state. "The residents of French Creek were surprised, and very agreeably so, to find that although neglected and forgotten by the Government they were of sufficient importance to bring a visitor from Victoria on a political mission. They had almost abandoned the idea of again exercising the privileges of the franchise as British subjects. Although numbering one-half of the electoral vote of the entire district, yet since '66 they had, to all intents and purposes been entirely disenfranchised."[9] Jessop's meeting there, reported a correspondent writing to the *Colonist,* was well attended. "After Mr. Jessop addressed the meeting, apparently with much acceptance, a resolution was unanimously passed, endorsing his views on Confederation, Responsible Government and the immediate adoption of the Canadian tariff."[10]

After what had seemed to Jessop an encouraging beginning of his campaign, it was necessary now to double back over the trail to the South Thompson. At Ducks he left it to turn south on the old fur-trader trail to the Okanagan. This took him through Grand Prairie. "This prairie is a very remarkable one, being surrounded by lofty hills and containing many thousand acres. Here and there a fir tree on its level, grassy surface, gives it a beautiful park-like appearance, reminding the traveller very forcibly as he descends the hill, of the 'Stately Homes of England'. The only farm at present on the prairie is occupied by Mr. Ingraham, but below this place there are several winter ranches for stock, it being considered one of the best localities in that part of the country for such a purpose."[11]

Following what is today the Vernon road, Jessop came with all the thrill of the tourist to the sun-drenched splendor of the Okanagan Valley. He was much impressed with the agricultural possibilities of this lovely region and wrote critically of the Government's neglect in not providing the area with adequate means of transportation or even mail service:

> With a fertile soil tolerably well watered, plenty of timber easily obtained, and unbounded pasturage, this district ought long ago to have been thickly settled by a farming and grazing population. From the head of the lake to Ellices' ranch at the outlet of the Okanagan river, a distance of eighty-five miles, there are about forty settlers, all of whom are more or less engaged in raising cattle, as no other branch of agricultural industry will pay. Dairy products, grain and vegetables are of no account whatever. Surplus milk, over and above what the calves can make use of is given to hogs. On many of the ranches cream is applied to the same purpose and the milk thrown away, and on others the new milk, even, is disposed of in like manner. Thus it is that dairy importations from Puget Sound, Oregon, California and the East drain the colony of hundreds of thousands of dollars when in the interior there is every facility for supplying all our demands were the population a thousand times more numerous than it really is . . . It is supposed that in the valleys of the Thompson and Okanagan, as far as Osoyoos, there are at least 15,000 head of cattle, all as fat as bunch grass can make them and increasing at the rate of 500 per year over and above the sales effected. Thus these valleys alone, were there proper facilities for so doing, would more than supply the entire colony with beef of the choicest description.
>
> Another grievance patiently endured by the Okanagan settlers is the want of mail communication. Messrs. O'Keefe, Greenbow and Wood whose extensive and well-stocked ranch is situated at the head of the Lake are under the necessity of sending to Duck and Pringles on the Thompson, a distance of forty or forty-five miles for letters or news from the outer world.[12]

Jessop was on his way now to Wild Horse Creek in the southeastern corner of British Columbia. To reach there from Osoyoos he could follow another Government trail, which, in defiance of topography, had been blazed across a succession of mountain ridges a few miles north of the international boundary. The present trans-provincial highway[13] follows quite closely this same route. Jessop followed the trail with one diversion where he dipped south into the United States following the Kettle River to Fort Colville and then heading northeast along the Columbia rejoined the Kootenay trail at Fort Sheppard on the Canadian side of the line. Here he had occasion to compare the cost of living on opposite sides of the boundary. At Fort Colville oats for his horse cost him three cents a pound as against twenty cents a pound at Fort Sheppard. South of the border "all is activity, prosperity and go-aheaditiveness; while north the withdrawing influence of Downing Street nips in the bud and effectively checks every attempt at opening up the resources of the country whether mineral or agricultural."[14] Confederation with Canada, he felt, would change all this. It offered the only hope for the future.

From Fort Sheppard on he found the Government trail very rough going and cursed its builders each step of the way:

> Leaving the Pen d'Oreill (sic), travelling becomes more and more difficult with now and then a steep descent. Burnt timber has, in many places, completely obliterated the trail for several miles to Goat River crossing. This is an impetuous torrent, not easily fordable at low water, and at higher stages very dangerous, or utterly impassable. At this much dreaded crossing the ascent of the notorious Sheppard Mountain fairly commences; and it is doubtful whether or not any worse trail can be found on the continent than the one traversing it. The corduroy was originally laid down without culverts, so that in some places the logs are altogether carried away by the water or are afloat on the surface of deep quagmires . . . It is absolute cruelty to animals to attempt to cross from Sheppard to Flat Bow Lake, even during August and September which are really the only two months in the year that the route is passable. How it happened that this trail was carried over the highest mountain in a mountain-peaked country is beyond comprehension.[15]

When he descended at last from this rugged terrain to the floor of the Kootenay Valley at Peavine Prairie[16] he was willing to forgive the trail-builders because "the sublimity of the scene is amply sufficient to repay (the traveller) for traversing nearly a fourth of the distance from the Pacific to the Atlantic seaboard." The park-like valley delighted him with its prairies of bunch grass interspersed with pines and set against the distant background of the snow-capped Rockies. "The Okanagan valley is scarcely superior to it in stockraising and farming capabilities. Were the deep diggings which are believed to exist on Wild Horse and other creeks developed and worked so as to maintain a larger and more permanent population and reasonable inducements held out by the government for the creation of flouring mills this would become a populous and highly remunerative agricultural district."[17]

Wild Horse Creek, Jessop's destination, was again a mining camp on the decline. Its heydey had been in 1863 and '64 when there had been about a thousand men there[18] but by 1870 most of them had moved out. J. C. Haynes, the District Magistrate making his rounds at the same time as Jessop visited Wild Horse, wrote that: "The place is nearly as dull as Rock Creek and I do not think there will be 50 white men in the district after another month".[19] The center for this small population was Fisherville about 50 miles north of the United States border. A few miles west of here on a stream flowing into the St. Mary River was Perry Creek, another mining camp with a few more eligible voters.

Jessop found on his arrival at Fisherville that there had been nine other candidates in addition to himself but that only one of these presented a serious challenge. This was R. J. Skinner. A Kootenay resident writing to the Victoria *Daily Standard* described the election campaign:[20]

The Government Express arrived here on the 7th inst. (November) and with it the writ for Election, also a gentleman from Victoria, Mr. John Jessop, a candidate for Legislative honors . . . Mr. R. J. Skinner, a clerk in the H. B. Co's store was asked to be a candidate, as it was understood that he intended wintering in Victoria, and the electors were generally pledged to support him before the arrival of Mr. Jessop, who, however, made a favorable impression.

On the day previous to the election, a meeting of the electors was held in Fisherville for the purpose of hearing the views of the candidates, the chair was occupied by Mr. John Galbraith, who stated the object of the meeting in an appropriate speech, and then introduced Mr. Jessop, who stated his views in reference to Confederation, Responsible Government, Tariff &c going minutely into it and showing a thorough acquaintance with the different subjects — he was followed by Mr. Skinner, who gave no uncertain sound in reference to the state of affairs now existing in the colony, promising to use his endeavors to defeat the 'trickery' of the present Government Officials and a reformation of matters in regard to Kootenay, advocating the appointment of a magistrate to reside permanently in the district, a monthly mail, improving the present trail, and the locating of a new road that would be open at any season of the year, all of which is much needed.

It is obvious from this correspondent that Jessop's appeal was centered on the broader national questions and Skinner's on the immediate and specific wants of that community. No one with any knowledge of rural politics could therefore doubt the outcome. Moreover, Jessop's Methodism and a long history of his active association with the temperance movement[21] was hardly likely to appeal to an electorate for whom liquor was thicker than water. But let Jessop describe the election himself:[22]

> The potent influence of 'Skinner Whiskey' which was flowing in the freest possible manner and had been for ten days previously, soon brought a number of its devotees to the polls — the undisguised support of the officials, constables particularly, together with all the aid the H.B.C. could muster — went in the same direction.

Polls were held only in Wild Horse and Perry Creeks. Not a vote was cast on the Big Bend where Jessop felt he had strong support. The returning officer had not bothered to stay there long enough to poll the residents. There were only two candidates nominated and only 54 votes cast — 40 for Skinner and 14 for Jessop.

Jessop returned to Victoria through Washington via Portland a sadder and a wiser man. His return trip was made in relative speed and comfort. He rode to Wallula at the junction of the Snake and Columbia where he connected with a Columbia River steamboat which took him to the Dalles; a fifteen mile railroad, then brought him again to a river steamboat. Farther downstream after another portage of five miles by railway at the Cascades and another interval by steamboat he reached Portland. From there he took the stage north to Olympia and from that port a ship brought him home to Victoria on the first of December. The return trip was accomplished in fifteen days. He had been travelling constantly for two months.

At home he settled down and wrote a long series of articles which appeared in the *Colonist* during December. They were entitled "Electioneering Tour of a Defeated Candidate."[23] In relating his experiences on the tour he could not refrain from complaining of the irregularities and injustices in the election. For disenfranchizing the Big Bend voters he blamed the Colonial officialdom. "The Government, when the writ for the election was dispatched to Kootenay, knew full well that the returning officer there would not remain long enough to poll the French Creek votes unless he had special instructions to that effect." He complained also about such irregularities in the polling at Wild Horse Creek as the lack of a secret ballot, the Deputy Returning Officer and the Poll Clerk both voting for Skinner, and American citizens in twelve instances, being allowed to vote.

His articles also served a constructive purpose to acquaint the population of the Island with the great potentialities lying dormant in the interior of their country. Victorians, then as now were a very insular folk, seeing the problems of British Columbia myopically as scarcely extending beyond the welfare of their own city and island. It was an eye-opening experience to Jessop to see the magnificent valleys of the Thompson, the Shuswap, the Okanagan and the Kootenay.

The last Legislative Council of British Columbia convened in January 1871 for the expressed purpose of considering the terms of union. There was little else for it to do although considerable debate ensued on the question of whether to bring responsible government before or after confederation. From the columns of the *Colonist* Jessop read with satisfaction that on January 20, the Council unanimously adopted an address to Queen Victoria praying for the adoption of union with Canada on the terms mutually agreed upon. These terms and Confederation were subsequently approved by the Canadian Parliament and finally British Columbia became the sixth province of the Dominion on July 20, 1871. Sir Leonard Tilley's prophetic dream of a dominion stretching "from sea to sea and from the river unto the ends of the earth" had become a reality.

Jessop now turned to the serious business of earning a living. His wife had been carrying on her own private school in the meantime and presumably Jessop had earned a little for his series of articles on "The Electioneering Tour of a Defeated Candidate". The public school situation had not improved. Neither the Government nor the Victoria school authorities had made any move to revive the defunct school system. Finally Jessop decided that he would reopen his own school. The *Colonist* of January 28, 1871 carried this announcement:

Central School

The Board of Education for Victoria City and District being unable, for the present, to reopen the Public School, Mr. J. Jessop begs to inform parents and guardians that he will reopen the CENTRAL SCHOOL, Lane at near Douglas on Wednesday next the 1st February.

The courses of study will compose the usual branches in English, together with Latin, Greek, Hebrew, French and instrumental music under thoroughly competent teachers.

The Girls' Department will be conducted by Mrs. Jessop at the ROSEVILLE ACADEMY, Yates Street.

TERMS — In the English branches, including vocal music $3 per month. The Classics, French and instrumental music will be charged as extras.

J. Jessop, Principal

During the spring months Jessop busied himself with his school. He was active also in Victoria's Agricultural and Horticultural Society, of which he was secretary. He was trying to interest the farming community in arranging what would have been British Columbia's first fair but he could arouse no enthusiasm at that time for the project.[24]

In June Graham Alston, who had held the purely honorary post of Inspector General of Schools, resigned to become the Attorney General of the West African colony of Sierra Leone. With his ambition still fixed on the superintendency of the school system, Jessop lost no time in applying to Governor Musgrave for the Inspector-Generalship. "In the future I hope to take an active part in promoting the interests of popular education in this my adopted country; and as as Inspector of Public Schools I should be in a better position than as a private citizen to ascertain the requirements of the colony and the suitability or otherwise of the present School Ordinance with a view of substituting something more in accordance with the progressive spirit of the age, and better adapted to the wants of the whole community, when the proper time arrives."[25] Musgrave's reply was a formal statement that Jessop would be considered for the position when the time should arrive for filling this appointment.

With the entry of British Columbia into the Dominion of Canada in July the new province had now to prepare for its first federal election to return six members to the House of Commons at Ottawa. One might have thought that having so recently tasted the bitter dregs of political defeat Jessop would not again seek elective office but he was, in his character, a peculiar combination of the enthusiastic optimist, the fighter, the idealist and the opportunist. Once more he tossed his hat into the ring and in July announced his candidacy for the federal riding of Vancouver which covered Vancouver Island except for Victoria District.[26]

Throughout the summer and fall months Jessop devoted himself wholeheartedly to the hustings. He travelled over the Island from Comox to Sooke, addressing meetings there and in Nanaimo, Saltspring Island, Maple Bay, Saanich and Cowichan. To audiences of fishermen, miners, farmers and loggers he stated his election platform simply and without equivocation. He supported the present Conservative Government of Sir John A. Macdonald. "Knowing the feasibility of the Canadian Pacific Railroad from personal observations along the greater part of the probable line of route and, having advocated such an enterprise in my Overland Journal published in Ontario, as well as on the coast for the last twelve years, I shall endeavor by every means in my power to bring that grand undertaking to a successful termination at Esquimalt or some other harbour on Vancouver Island."[27] While desiring to encourage immigration he was, however, against importing coolie labour for the railway or other public works. If elected he would tour the Eastern Canadian cities lecturing on the Past, Present and Future of British Columbia. He pledged himself to work for a dry dock at some Island port, possibly Nanaimo. The Canadian tariff policy had his support. From his experience in the Kootenay election he wanted to see introduced a secret ballot at all Federal, Provincial and Municipal elections. Telegraphy, lighthouses, harbor improvements, hospitals, asylums, prisons, fisheries, and geological surveys were some of the many topics over which his interest ranged.

Jessop's opponent was the Victoria merchant Robert Wallace. The *Colonist*, supporting Jessop, left its readers in no doubt that the schoolmaster would win the election hands down. The *Standard*, Victoria's other newspaper, supported Wallace and was equally certain that its candidate would be the victor. When all the results were finally announced Wallace had won by 131 votes to Jessop's 101.[28] Thus ended the political career of John Jessop.

In January 1872 a rumor from the Birdcages that a paid office of Inspector of Schools might soon be created prompted Jessop to put pen to paper again and send off an application for this position to the province's first Lieutenant Governor, Joseph W. Trutch. Nothing came of it at the time but a formal acknowledgement.[29]

Once more in February Jessop and Burr presented their petition for the recovery of salary arrears. "We are fully aware that we have no legal claim upon the Government; but the School Board, having no money for educational purposes at its disposal, nor any means of obtaining it, recommended us to apply to the Legislative Assembly for relief. All your petitioners ask for is that the matter may be thoroughly examined by the Assembly or a Committee thereof, or in any way that your Excellency may see fit to adopt." The Executive Council did consider the petition but did nothing for the teachers.[30]

To Jessop it must have seemed like the end of the line — a final rejection — but the fulfilment of his ambition was soon to come.

FOOTNOTES

[1] The Legislative Council consisted of 22 members, 13 of whom were nominated by the Governor and 9 elected. The Governor was his own Prime Minister.

[2] Shelton, George, *British Columbia and Confederation,* University of Victoria, 1967, p. 85.

[3] Hankin to Buckingham, March 11, 1870, in *B.C. Historical Quarterly* XIII, 1, January 1949, p. 37.

[4] Waites, K. A., "Responsible Government and Confederation", *B.C. Historical Quarterly,* VI, 2, April 1942, p. 119.

[5] *Colonist,* September 30, 1870, p. 3. John Robson took over the editorship of the *Colonist* on July 1, 1869 when David Higgins, proprietor of the *Colonist,* purchased the *British Columbian* plant and hired Robson as political editor.

[6] Jessop, John, "Electioneering Tour of a Defeated Candidate", *Colonist,* December 8, 1870, p. 3.

[7] Balf, Mary, *Kamloops, A History of the District Up to 1914,* Kamloops Museum Association, p. 42.

[8] Jessop, *op. cit.,* December 9, 1870, p. 3.

[9] *Ibid.,* December 9, p. 3.

[10] *Colonist,* December 18, 1870, p. 3.

[11] Jessop, *op cit.,* December 11, 1870, p. 3. Ingraham was an American who owned the last of the Cariboo camels that had been used to pack supplies to the Cariboo. The community that grew up here was first called Grande Prairie and since 1926, Westwold. See Mary Balf, *op. cit.,* pp. 136-138.

[12] *Ibid.,* p. 3. The pioneer ranch at O'Keefe's has been converted into a most interesting museum of the early days.

[13] Highway number 3. This trail was an extension of the one from Hope to the Similkameen.

[14] Jessop, *op. cit.,* December 13, 1870, p. 2.

[15] *Ibid.,* p. 2.

[16] North of present day Cranbrook.

[17] Jessop, *op. cit.,* December 15, 1870, p. 2.

[18] White, Hester E., "John Carmichael Haynes", *B.C. Historical Quarterly,* IV, 3, July 1940, p. 189.

[19] *Ibid.,* p. 197.

[20] "Kootenay Correspondence", Victoria *Daily Standard,* December 12, 1870, p. 2.

[21] Waddington's Journal, September 7, 1865. Listed among Jessop's credentials is a letter from Sir Oliver Mowat stating that Jessop had been actively associated with the temperance movement in 1859. B.C. Archives.

[22] Jessop, *op cit.,* December 17, 1870, p. 3.

[23] *Colonist,* December 8, 9, 11, 13, 15, 17 and 20, 1870.

[24] *Colonist,* October 1870, p. 3., and May 1871, p. 3.

[25] Jessop to Musgrave, June 14, 1871.

[26] The ridings were Cariboo, New Westminster, Vancouver, Yale and Victoria (which had two M.P.s).

[27] *Colonist,* September 12, 1871, p. 2.

[28] *Colonist,* December 8, 1871, p. 3 and December 24, 1871, p. 3.

[29] Jessop to Trutch, January 4, 1872. B.C. Archives.

[30] Jessop and Burr to Trutch, February 19, 1872.

CHAPTER SEVEN

Superintendent Jessop

The first government of the Province of British Columbia was formed in November 1871. The newly appointed Lieutenant Governor was Joseph W. Trutch (later Sir Joseph). There was as yet in the province no such thing as a party system but it would have seemed a safe assumption that the Lieutenant Governor would choose one of the two prominent leaders of the confederation movement to head his first government. Instead Trutch invited John Foster McCreight, an Irish lawyer representing Victoria, to form the first administration. British Columbia's first premier had never sat in an elected legislature before and possessed little tolerance for the parliamentary process. He selected only two others for his cabinet, Alexander Rocke Robertson, the member from Esquimalt as Provincial Secretary and Henry Holbrook, the member from New Westminster, as Chief Commissioner of Lands and Works.

For the past two years the general public had been expecting its first provincial government to do something about the deplorable state of the school system. A new Public Schools Bill, therefore, must necessarily be prepared and placed before the first session of the Legislative Assembly. The Cabinet minister whose responsibilities according to Canadian custom, would include education was the Provincial Secretary.[1] Robertson turned for advice and assistance in drafting this new bill to John Jessop whose advocacy of a free non-sectarian school system was widely known. Together they designed the bill which would restore free schools and establish a pattern for a public educational system which, with many modifications, is that of the present day.[2] They drew liberally upon the Ontario School legislation of Ryerson as their model.

The new school bill was ready for the committee stage in early spring and went through its three readings in March. Although objecting to the restrictions governing the appointment of the Superintendent, the Lieutenant Governor gave it the royal assent on April 11.

The Public School Act of 1872[3] repealed the previous school legislation of the colony and provided for the province a simple structure of provincial and local authorities, defining their duties and functions. A Board of Education, "six fit and proper persons", was to be appointed by the Lieutenant Governor and to hold office during his pleasure. The Lieutenant Governor was to appoint a Superintendent of Education also to hold office during his pleasure. The restrictions to which Trutch had objected remained in the act and stipulated that "no person shall be eligible for Superintendent unless he has been an experienced and successful teacher of at least five years' standing, and holds a first class certificate from some College, School, or Board of Examination in some other Province or County where a Public School System has been in operation." The Superintendent would be ex officio Chairman of the Board of Education.

The duties of this Board of Education were all-embracing to do everything necessary "to advance the interests and usefulness of Public Schools" and to establish Rules and Regulations for them. It was to "select, adopt and prescribe a uniform series of textbooks" and to purchase and take charge of all school apparatus and equipment. It could, if it deemed it expedient, establish in any district "a separate school for females", presided over by a female teacher or teachers" — a concession to the feelings of many parents of the Victorian Age who feared the influence of rough young males on the innocence and femininity of their daughters. The Board was also given authority, when and where it deemed expedient, to establish High Schools "wherein the classics, mathematics and higher Branches of Education shall be taught." Finally this body was the sole authority to examine, certificate and appoint all teachers and to fix their salaries.

The Superintendent was required to visit each school in the province at least once a year and report on its progress, attendance, maintenance and management, to see that only the authorized textbooks were used, and to make annually a report on the state of the province's schools to the Lieutenant Governor. He could suspend the certificate of any teacher pending action of the Board. He was to distribute and be responsible for the payment of all provincial grants to the schools.

One of his duties, inspired no doubt by Ryerson's belief in the importance of "selling" the cause of education to the general public was the stipulation that he was "to deliver, in each School District, at least once a year, a public lecture on some subject connected with the objects, principles and means of practical education and to do all in his power to persuade and animate parents, guardians, trustees and teachers to improve the character and efficiency of the Public Schools, and to secure the sound education of the young generally."

The salary of the superintendent was set by the act at two thousand dollars per annum with additional allowances for travelling expenses.

For the first time in British Columbia the citizens of a school district were empowered and required to elect a local board of school trustees, three in number and holding office normally for three years.[4] An annual school meeting had to be held in each school district to elect the trustees and to hear their report on school business. It would seem, after considering the very extensive powers of the Provincial Board of Education, that there could be little left for the local boards to do. They were, however, charged with the responsibilities of accounting for all school moneys and disbursing the salary grants to the teachers. In their hands was placed the custody and safekeeping of all school property, its repair and maintenance. They were also empowered to visit their school from time to time to see that the school laws and regulations were being carried out. Annually in January each local board was to send a report on its school district to the Superintendent of Education.

The act also defined the duties of the teachers in such familiar terms as "to teach diligently and faithfully all the branches required to be taught in the school," to keep a careful record of the pupils and their attendance and a visitor's book.[5] They were to "maintain proper order and discipline" in the schools and to hold at the end of each half-year a public examination.

The nonsectarian principle of public education, well established in colonial days, was re-stated in the new act: "All Public Schools established under the provisions of this Act, shall be conducted upon strictly nonsectarian principles. The highest morality shall be inculcated, but no religious dogmas or creed shall be taught."

Nowhere did the act specifically require that all public schools should be free except by implication. The Government was to set apart waste lands for school purposes where necessary in each school district and to grant, on the application of the local school board, endorsed by the Superintendent of Education, whatever funds might be required for teachers' salaries, erecting or renting a school house and furnishing it. These grants would come from a Public School

Fund derived from the general revenues of the Province and initially to be $40,000. There was therefore no requirement of local property taxation or other local revenues or fees to help finance the schools.

Writing in 1895, an early observer of the British Columbia scene, J. B. Kerr, stated that Rocke Robertson, "aided by Mr. Jessop, introduced and passed a School Act similar in most of its provisions to that then in force in Ontario."[6] There were certainly many parallels between the school legislation of the two provinces. Both had General Boards of Education, local elected three-trustee boards and Superintendents with similar powers appointed by the Lieutenant Governors. The British Columbia Act in adopting "a uniform series of textbooks" was following Ryerson's precedent with the National series which had originated in Ireland. In giving the General Board authority to establish "High Schools", rather than the traditional term "Grammar Schools", the British Columbia act was borrowing the new term from Ontario Legislation of 1871 which brought the old semi-independent Grammar Schools into the public system as "High Schools." Annual reports, public examinations, lectures by the Superintendent (and in Ontario by District Superintendents), provisions for a group of special "school visitors" and the statements regarding the duties of teachers were noticeable parallels.

There were, however, certain marked differences — first and foremost being that the British Columbia system was a unified non-sectarian one with no provision (as in Ontario) for separate schools for the Roman Catholic minority. The provision of separate public schools for girls was unique to British Columbia and more specifically to the larger centres of Victoria, New Westminster and Nanaimo. Victoria, indeed, clung to its separate Boys' Central and Girls' Central Schools until 1937.[7] The newness of British Columbia, the paucity and scattered character of its population could account for other differences as, for example, the lack of District Superintendents and of teacher-training facilities.

The new office of Superintendent of Education was now a most tempting position, offering power, prestige and, for those times, a respectable salary. To Jessop it represented the goal of a lifetime and it was only to be expected that he would make every effort to win it. Having had a hand in launching the ship, it was not strange that he might want to take the helm.

He made formal application for the position in March, first by writing to Rocke Robertson.[8] Shortly thereafter he considered it necessary to write personally to Premier McCreight. In this letter, after stating his qualifications in training and experience for the position, he felt it necessary to add a defense of his name against certain malicious rumors:[9]

A report, intended no doubt, to prejudice my interests, was circulated a short time since, that my certificate of qualification as a teacher was revoked — I beg to say most emphatically that *such is not the case.*

It seems that the restrictive amendment to clause 4 of the School Act is not looked upon with favour by the Lieut. Governor and others — I hope that neither his Excellency, yourself nor other members of the Cabinet will entertain the idea for a moment that I had anything whatever to do with that matter; and that my prospects will not suffer for what I had no hand in originating or carrying through the House.

As vigorous efforts are being made in certain quarters to induce the government to overlook my claims, I now ask for them your favourable consideration, this being the only position in the Educational Department of British Columbia that I shall ever seek for or accept.

His plea was successful. On April 17 the Government appointed him to the position at the salary of $2,000. The *Colonist* in announcing the appointment observed that, "Mr. Jessop is a very old resident and an experienced teacher and made sacrifices to preserve the old Island Free School system that ought to entitle him to the everlasting gratitude of those parents whose children were benefitted by these sacrifices. The appointee is in every respect worthy of the appointment and the Ministry have acted wisely in making the selection."[10] It seems to have been a popular appointment. No doubt Jessop had enemies but he also had many friends. One such, a teacher at the Sumass school in the Fraser Valley, wrote to congratulate him with more sincerity perhaps than literary facility: "It affords me much pleasure to hear of your appointment as the Superintendent of Education. I hope you success and pray that you may have wisdom from the great Sorce of all knowledge to establish and conduct the educational affairs of this land." He ended by inviting Jessop to a Methodist Camp Meeting.[11]

Jessop called the first meeting of the new Provincial Board of Education on May 7, 1872. The "six fit and proper persons" were Dr. W. F. Tolmie, M. W. T. Drake, E. Marvin, R. Williams, A. J. Langley and A. Munro. They lost no time in proceeding to revive and put in order the school system of the province. All teachers presently holding certificates had these temporarily confirmed and all seeking appointments were advised to present themselves to the Education Office with their testimonials to be examined by the Board.

A list of textbooks was officially approved, all of which were books in use in Ontario schools, and Jessop was authorized to order them from Campbell and Sons, publishers of Toronto. They were to be sold to the pupils through the schools at the Ontario retail prices. The first provincial textbook list included the *Canadian Series* of five Readers, the Canadian Spelling Book, Smith and McMurchy's *Elementary Advanced Arithmetics, Easy Lessons in Geography,* by J. G. Hodgins, Ryerson's assistant, Campbell's *Modern School Geography and Atlas,* Lennies' *English Grammar,* Colenso's *Algebra,* Young's *Euclid,* Johnson's *Bookkeeping,* and Collier's *General History of the British Empire.*[12] The inclusion of Algebra, Geometry and Bookkeeping in the elementary school curriculum in those days may surprise the modern reader but both in Ontario and in British Columbia the elementary school teacher, in the absence of high schools, ventured often to give his senior pupils some introduction to high school subjects.

School attendance had always been very irregular in the early schools. The Board now took stern measures to combat this by making the teachers responsible for the attendance of their pupils. A resolution of the Board stated that if three-quarters of the students in a school district did not attend school this would be grounds for the dismissal of the teacher. A signed statement from the parent accounting for the child not attending school would, however, absolve the teacher.[13]

Opening and closing exercises were adopted by the Board. Although the schools were to be officially nonsectarian certain prayers were authorized, including the Lord's Prayer, and the Ten Commandments were to be taught. However, on the express wish of parents, children could be excused from such exercises.[14]

In July the Board finally settled the claims of teachers to their long-awaited arrears in salary and paid them up to the end of March 1872. At least there was enough money in the School Fund to pay salary grants regularly.

In the meantime Jessop had established an Education Office in rented premises on Government Street provided by the Chief Commissioner of Lands and Works and here he carried on single-handed the business of his Department. For the full period of his service as Superintendent he had no clerical assistance whatsoever. He read and answered by his own hand all his correspondence which mounted in time to six or seven hundred letters per year. In such a highly centralized system there was no delegation of authority. All purchases of texts and equipment and the distribution of such were made by him even to the extent of carrying parcels personally to the steamboats to see them off to some school up-Island or across the strait. He was responsible for the disbursement each month of salary cheques to teachers, for preparing and conducting qualifying examinations for teachers, transacting routine business, visiting and inspecting schools and giving his annual lectures in each district. With so much to do, he resented, as unnecessarily bureaucratic, a requirement that he submit semi-monthly to the Provincial Secretary a report on all his activities.[15]

There are only two photographs of Jessop known to exist, one taken in retirement in later life, and the other dating from about this time. It shows the small group of officials that constituted the Province's first civil service. They are posed on the steps of the old parliament buildings — the "Birdcages." Jessop appears as perhaps the most dapper member of the group — still young, in his early forties, of medium height, spare, with high cheek bones, a strong nose, moustache and a small goatee.

Under the School Act the Superintendent was required to submit an annual report on the school system "on or before the first of September." Largely statistical, it was to report the numbers attending the schools of the province, the average attendance, the "branches taught", expenditures, the teachers and their qualifications and the number of visits made by the Superintendent to inspect the schools.

In the three months since his appointment to the end of the school year (July 31) Jessop had scarcely time to survey and assess his school system and compile a complete report by the September deadline. Nevertheless he did present a shorter one to the Lieutenant Governor in August.[16] It included "a brief retrospect of what had been accomplished before the present School Act came into force" in which he traced the development of public schools from 1855 to the debacle of 1870. He proceeded to summarize what his Department had done since its inception in prescribing rules and regulations for the schools, in adopting textbooks, and in setting certification standards for teachers. He concluded by giving detailed reports on those schools he had been able to visit in the first three months of his incumbency.

As might be expected, most of them were on Vancouver Island. The city of Victoria had two public schools, each with two teachers. The Boys' School under Colin C. McKenzie, B.A., assisted by Mr. John Mundell, was held in the old Colonial School at the head of Yates Street on the ten-acre School Reserve. It had an enrolment of 108 boys. The Girls' School under Mrs. Sarah Hayward assisted by Miss Margaret J. Baxter met in premises on Broughton Street near Government. Its enrolment was not reported. Both schools, wrote Jessop, had recently been "fitted up".

What had happened to Jessop's own Central School building and to his wife's private school is not known. Presumably Jessop sold the premises on Fort Street and there is no further record of Mrs. Jessop's private academy for young ladies.[17]

Jessop apologized for the brevity of his first Annual Report. He had yet to see this extensive province, to learn what schools were operating, what children were without the opportunity of attending schools and what could be done about it. He was ready to start off on his first inspectoral tour of the province, after which he promised the Lieutenant Governor he would submit a supplementary report.

FOOTNOTES

[1] British Columbia did not have a Minister of Education until 1891.

[2] *The Canadian Album: Men of Canada,* Vol. IV, Brantford, Bradley, Garretsen & Co. 1895, p. 87. Also Kerr, J. B., *op. cit.,* p. 208. Both these sources state that Jessop helped frame the act.

[3] An Act Respecting Public Schools, 1872.

[4] Under the Vancouver Island School Act of 1865 the Governor was given authority to appoint local boards but he did not do so. Under the Common School Ordinance of 1869, the Government could (but not must) provide for the establishment and election of Local Boards.

[5] "All Judges, Clergymen, Members of the Legislature and others interested in education, shall be school visitors." (Section 35).

[6] Kerr, J. B., *op. cit.,* p. 208.

[7] Johnson, F. H., *A History of Public Education in British Columbia,* Vancouver, U.B.C. Publications Centre, 1964, p. 51.

[8] Jessop to A. R. Robertson, 15 March, 1872, B.C. Archives.

[9] Jessop to J. F. McCreight, 26 March, 1872, B.C. Archives.

[10] *Colonist,* April 18, 1872, p. 3.

[11] A. C. Peers to J. Jessop, Sumass, April 24, 1872, B.C. Archives.

[12] First Annual Report on the Public Schools of British Columbia, Victoria, 1872, p. 2.

[13] Minutes of the Board of Education, June 7, 1872. B.C. Archives.

[14] *Ibid.,* June 18, 1872.

[15] Jessop, John, Letter-Book Correspondence Outward 1872-73, Ap. 26, 1873, to Provincial Secretary, B.C. Archives. John Ash had succeeded Robertson as Provincial Secretary in January 1873.

[16] First Annual Report on the Public Schools in the Province of British Columbia for the Year Ending July 31, 1872.

[17] Twelve denominational and private schools are listed as operating in Victoria in 1872-73. There is no mention of Mrs. Jessop's school among them. (Journals of the Legislative Assembly. Session 1872-73, Appendix G to First Annual Report of the Superintendent of Education.)

CHAPTER EIGHT

Tour Of Inspection

One of the duties required of the Superintendent under the Public School Act was "to visit each Public School within his jurisdiction once in each year at least." On such official visits he was "to examine . . . the state and condition of the school as respects the progress of the pupils in learning, the order and discipline observed, the system of instruction pursued, the mode of keeping the school registers, the average attendance of pupils, the character and condition of the buildings and premises and to give such advice as he may judge proper." Nor was this all. It will be recalled that the Act required him to deliver, in each community that he visited, an annual lecture on the theme of public education. Presumably this was to be, in part at least, inspirational "to persuade and animate parents, guardians, trustees, and teachers to improve the character and efficiency of the Public Schools, and to secure the sound education of the young generally."[1]

When one considers the primitive travelling conditions of the time and the great distances to be covered, the Superintendent's annual tour of inspection took on something of the magnitude of a combined marathon and talkathon.

Jessop decided to divide the project into a spring tour on the Island and Lower Mainland and a fall tour of the Interior. Spring would be an excellent time for visiting the schools of the Island and Lower Fraser Valley because transportation to and from these places could be by steamboat or canoe and he could finish these school districts before the summer vacations. For touring the Interior schools only one season was suitable — the autumn. In spring the unpaved roads were quagmires of mud; in winter they were often impassable with snow drifts.

He started off his spring tour on June 10, 1872, by boarding the steamer *Enterprise* at the old Hudson's Bay Company wharf. Owned and operated by the H.B.C., *Enterprise* was a graceful side-wheeler on the regular run between Victoria and New Westminster. As the steamer paddled its way up the muddy Fraser followed by streamers of black smoke Jessop must have wondered just what was the state of the schools after the recent years of neglect. There had been few reports available, none from most places. Were they still closed down or had the teachers returned to them and what were the new school boards doing?

From New Westminster he proceeded up the river to Langley. His inspectoral diary has this comment:[2]

> June 12th. Visited Langley by str. *Onward* — No school since last month — Late teacher as anxious to leave as the settlers are that he should do so — thought it better not to institute an investigation into the late difficulties; but to recommend the removal of Mr. Kennedy — Travelled over the district on both sides of the Fraser — No possibility of re-opening school till August on account of mosquitoes — School house in very good order with comfortable dwelling attached; but no maps or blackboard — Good well with pump in it — put there by the late teacher and should be paid for — About 40 children in the district — Returned to New Westminster in canoe.

The next day he was off for the settlements on Burrard Inlet. To reach these he would have hired a horse and ridden over the old trail now followed by the Douglas Road from New Westminster, passing Deer Lake to come out on the south shore of Burrard Inlet near the present Vancouver Exhibition Grounds. There were two sawmilling settlements on the Inlet at this time, one on the north shore at Moody's Mill (or Moodyville) and the other at the village of Granville or Hasting's Mill on the south shore. These sawmill communities, situated in clearings surrounded by the dense rainforest, were the humble beginnings of what later were to be the cities of North Vancouver and Vancouver. In February the Hastings Mill manager, Captain Raymur, had provided a little frame building for Vancouver's first school. It stood among the raw stumps and slashings of the recent clearing operations.

Jessop chose to visit the north shore first, taking a boat across the inlet. His diary reads:[3]

> June 13. Started for Burrard Inlet at 7 a.m. Visited School taught by Miss Haynes at Moody and Co's Mills — Found 16 children in attendance — 9 girls and 7 boys — School orderly

and quiet — Classes merely beginning — Reading and Spelling not good — But little Arithmetic and Geography — No Grammar — Writing just commenced by 7 or 8 children — School-room small, but with a little alteration might answer for some time to come — Erected and furnished by firm — No maps or blackboard — About 25 children in district.

Jessop made no mention of the fact that the Moodyville school was "in such close proximity to the refuse burner of the mill that sometimes the teacher and children were smoked out of their little school-house."[4]

In the afternoon he crossed over to Granville. Here he noted:

Female teacher urgently required — School house large and comfortable, put up by the Firm and used as a church — Good stove in the building which Capt. Raymur thinks ought to be paid for out of school funds — The harmonium might be used for school purposes — Desks required — About 25 children of school age in the district — the trustees, manager and parents anxious that Miss Sweney should be appointed teacher . . .

The next day he was back in New Westminster inspecting its school, taught by the man who had supported him in the Victoria teachers' strike:

June 14. Visited Public School in New Westminster taught by Mr. W. H. Burr — Thirty-three children in attendance — of those 7 were girls — Reading and spelling to 4th Book of lessons very good — Arithmetic moderately so — pupils in simple rules only — Grammar not far advanced nor very good as far as the class has gone. Geography Class not at all creditable — Writing good.

He found the school "orderly and quiet" and commented that the school house was "the best in the Province, but somewhat out of repair." It had no blackboards but was well supplied with maps and charts. It was being organized into a boys' department and a girls' department, the latter under Miss M. Glyde.

Having inspected these lower mainland centres, Jessop returned to Victoria and a fortnight later was off to visit the schools "up-Island". His first stop was Saltspring Island, where there was a large settlement of negroes, mostly freedmen, who had come to the colony in the 1850's to escape discrimination in the United States. The teacher, Mr. J. C. Jones, was himself a negro who had attended the

University of Ohio.[5] Jessop found him "itinerating between the Middle and Northern settlements," an unnecessary waste of time in Jessop's view because "none of the children are more than three miles from the School-house and the road is improving year by year. There are 25 children of school age in the two settlements above referred to, of whom seven reside in the northern and sixteen in the middle settlement." On the day he visited the school in the Northern settlement he found only two girls and a boy in attendance. "The boy was working in Latin Grammar, having become such a proficient in English Grammar and Geography that those studies were dropped a year ago and Latin substituted! So the teacher reported. An examination in those branches and arithmetic did not by any means establish the fact of former proficiency." He noted that "an interesting and thriving settlement" was developing between Burgoyne Bay and Fulford Harbour in the south of Saltspring Island and that an application had recently been made for a school there.[6]

The entry in Jessop's diary for the next day reads: "June 29 — went to Nanaimo by canoe — rained heavily — arrived at 6:20 p.m."[7] Nanaimo at this time was a town of seven to eight hundred population, all dependent upon the coal mine which was producing about thirty thousand tons of coal a year. There was some agriculture in the neighborhood. A Nova Scotian visitor in 1872 described Nanaimo as not looking like a coal-mining town. "The houses are much above the average of miners' residences in Britain or Nova Scotia. They are scattered about, often in picturesque situations, with gardens, and not in long, mean, soot-covered rows, laid out with the idea that men who see nothing of beauty underground cannot be expected to appreciate it above."[8]

The school in Nanaimo had remained in operation throughout the recent "lean years". In spite of the government grants being cut off in the last years of the Colony the school had carried on by charging fees. "Thus," according to this city's historian, "Nanaimo has the longest record of continuous operation of any school in the province."[9] Mr. J. C. Young was in charge of the school and a Miss McLeod had just been appointed to the Girls' Department. Jessop was not impressed by the school.[10] The children were not punctual but kept dropping in throughout the day until 26 had arrived. "Children somewhat disorderly, and but little attention paid to the teacher. Discipline and arrangement of studies very deficient. For want of books a large class, not far enough advanced for Third Reader were reading in the

Fifth." He found the pupils deficient in all subjects. "The school room of the worst possible description."

While in Nanaimo he took the opportunity to cross over to Gabriola Island where the settlers were wishing to establish a school. He met them and noted that there were 15 or 16 children of school age there but living in two settlements rather far apart.

On July 3 he reached Comox, the northernmost point on his Island tour. Here he found no school in operation, "the teacher, Mr. Rees, having resigned, when the building used as a school house, which belongs to the Episcopal Church, was required for Mission purposes." After making arrangements for a new school house to be built here and the school reopened, Jessop returned to Victoria his spring tour completed.

During the summer months Jessop was busy catching up with the unattended business and accumulated correspondence of his Department and in preparing his first Annual Report. As August drew to a close he was ready to start off again on his autumn tour of the schools of the Interior. The *Colonist* of August 30 carried a brief announcement to the effect that "J. Jessop Esq., Superintendent of Education, leaves by the *Enterprise* this morning for an official tour through the Mainland part of the Province where he will inspect the existing schools and take the necessary steps for providing schools where they do not already exist. He will probably be absent about a month."[11]

Jessop was now able to travel in style to the Interior — at least to the extent of enjoying what comforts were then available to the travelling public. The river steamboat *Onward* brought him from New Westminster to Yale, taking two days bucking the swift current to make these 95 miles. (It sometimes did the return trip in six hours.) At Yale he took the famous Barnard's Express (or the BX as it was commonly called) northward to the Cariboo. The first hundred miles of the trip from Yale to Cache Creek was still an adventure as the stage with its six spirited horses clattered and swayed over that spectacular road and the traveller, from his seat of honor beside the driver, looked down at the swirling jade-green waters of the river hundreds of feet below. At the end of each day's run the driver brought his team up in a final dashing gallop before one of the road-houses where home-cooked meals and comfortable beds awaited the dusty, weary traveller and mountains of oats and a well-kept stable rewarded the foam-flecked horses.

In the morning, after a gargantuan breakfast of oatmeal covered with thick cream, a large steak with fried potatoes, two or three fried eggs, coffee and hot cakes (and sometimes pie) the travellers mounted the stage and with the crack of the driver's whip were off again on the next lap of the journey. The hospitality of these inns or "milehouses" was one of the greatly appreciated amenities of travelling in the early days of the Interior. Their charges were reasonable, fifty to seventy-five cents for a bed and the same price for a meal.[12]

From Cache Creek it took four days by stage to cover the 275 miles to the Williams Creek - Barkerville area which Jessop reached on September 9. He found that the school there had closed and that the number of school-age children had dwindled to ten in and around Barkerville. "With so few children, it became a question as to whether the school should be re-opened; but finding there a comfortable and well-furnished little school house, in good order, and much anxiety expressed on the part of the parents that their children should not lose all the advantages accruing from the faithful year's work rendered by Mr. Mundell (the previous teacher), it was thought advisable to do so; and on the recommendation of the School Trustees, Mrs. J. Hall was temporarily appointed teacher, subject to the approval of the Board of Education, at a salary of $50 per month."[13]

From the time of his appointment as Superintendent, Jessop had been turning over in his mind the problem of providing free schooling for the children living in the many small mining and ranching communities of this vast Interior region. There were often too few families to make up the minimum of fifteen children aged five to sixteen required by the School Act for opening a new school district. Mining communities, by their very nature, were unstable and their populations rose and fell like the barometer. He had already evolved a plan which might offer a solution to this problem of a thinly distributed population. He would not try to take schools to these children but bring the children to a school. He would establish several central boarding schools, maintained by the Government at minimal costs to parents and bring the children from a wide area in to these. In his first Annual Report in August he had already proposed consideration of "the advisability of establishing a system of Boarding Schools, as a means of saving expenditure, in districts where population is scattered, so as to bring educational advantages within reach of a large number of settlers who otherwise would be deprived of

92

them."[14] He had recently met and discussed this idea with the Rev. J. B. Good of Lytton who was an enthusiastic supporter of the idea.

Before leaving the Williams Creek - Barkerville district Jessop had to give the first of his annual public lectures and this afforded him the opportunity to launch his Boarding School proposal. His method on this and subsequent occasions was to discuss the proposal first with the school trustees or local citizens and if they approved of the idea, have them primed with a motion to place before the public meeting. On this occasion Jessop shared the platform in Barkerville with the local members of both provincial and national parliaments. There was a large audience and the meeting was fully reported by the *Cariboo Sentinel*.[15] After some long-winded political speeches, "Mr. Jessop, the Superintendent of Education, was then introduced to the meeting by the chairman. In a clear and lucid speech, which he said he felt compelled to curtail owing to the lateness of the evening, after setting forth the advantages of education and the liberal provisions made in regard to it by the Legislature, he invited the audience to express their views and wishes in respect of their local school.

Mr. Thompson, M.P., then came forward and moved, and Mr. Barnston (M.P.P.) seconded the following resolution:

That in order to meet the educational wants of the sparsely populated districts of this Province, it is the opinion of this meeting that one or more Boarding Schools should be established in some convenient locality or localities, the buildings to be erected and the educational department provided by Government — parents and guardians to contribute a reasonable sum for defraying their children's board.

The resolution was "carried unanimously."

At each public meeting he held from then on throughout this inspectoral tour similar resolutions were engineered by Jessop, presented and carried. Such was the spontaneity of democracy in action!

From Barkerville Jessop turned south to visit Clinton where he found the teacher, Miss McWha, teaching twelve children, all beginners, in an upstairs apartment "kindly given by Mr. Wadhams for the purpose; no accommodation for writing, nor are there any other necessary requisites for a school room. The acting Trustee Board have, however, decided on erecting a school house at once, so that presumably by the time winter sets in, the teacher and pupils will be comfortably provided for."[16]

His next official visit was to Lillooet where he found that no school had been opened, although there were sixteen children of school age "within a few rods of the Court House, and as many more in the surrounding District."

At Lytton also the school had been closed for a year. As there were seventeen children of school age he arranged for the appointment of a teacher, Mrs. J. B. Good, the Anglican minister's wife, at a salary of fifty dollars per month.

From Lytton he decided to strike east and visit the Thompson Country and the Okanagan. This time he went by horseback through the sunlit Nicola Valley. There was no school here but at Nicola Lake he held a meeting of the settlers at which he broached the proposal for a centralized Boarding School. They too expressed agreement by a formal resolution.

In Kamloops Jessop stayed with John Tait, the agent in charge of the Hudson's Bay post.[17] The fur trade had long since ceased to bring in any appreciable returns here but Fort Kamloops had been important to the Hudson's Bay Company because of its large horse ranch which, in the days of the fur trade, had provided the pack horse trains to transport the furs down from the Interior posts, through the Thompson and Okanagan Valleys to Fort Vancouver for shipment overseas. Now Tait's five hundred horses were a drug on the market and he was trying to sell them off at bargain prices.

Kamloops in 1872 was a small community consisting of the Hudson's Bay post at its western end, a couple of stores, a so-called "hotel", a jail and Court House and a dozen or so other buildings strung out in line along the south bank of the Thompson. A mile to the north was an Indian village, at Tranquille Fortune's grist mill and in the general area a scattering of ranches. A sleepy little hamlet beside its placid river, it gazed across at the great lion-coloured mass of Mount Paul, apparently content that the world should pass it by.

But just at this point in time the modern age reached out to touch the town. Sandford Fleming's party which had been exploring across Canada and through the Yellowhead Pass route for the projected Canadian Pacific Railway, after a long and arduous transcontinental journey from Halifax, was coming down the North Thompson. On September 28, the very day that Jessop was in Kamloops, the party arrived. Dr. George M. Grant, Fleming's secretary who described their

Hastings Mill in 1872, the sawmill settlement which was the beginning of Vancouver. The school is the second building from the right. Vancouver Archives.

The "Birdcages", the old colonial parliament buildings in Victoria in 1884. From "The West Shore" — B.C. Archives.

The first civil service of the Province of British Columbia. Jessop is standing on the first step, behind the fourth and fifth men of the front row. Taken on the steps of the "Birdcages", the colonial parliament building, in the early 1870's. B.C. Archives.

The Victoria Central School, the first brick school in British Columbia, built in 1875. The first high school is the building in its rear. B.C. Archives.

historic journey in his book *Ocean to Ocean* recorded the occasion:[18]

> The boat was hauled in to the bank; and Trutch went up to the Fort. Mr. Tait the agent, at once came down, and with a genuine H.B., which is equivalent to a Highland, welcome, invited us to take up our quarters with him. Gladly accepting the hospitable offer, we were soon seated in a comfortable room beside a glowing fire. We were at Kamloops! beside a Post Office, and a waggon road; and in the adjoining room, the half-dozen heads of families resident in or near Kamloops were holding a meeting with the Provincial Superintendent of Education, to discuss the best means of establishing a school. Surely we had returned to civilization and the ways of men!

The outcome of the meeting mentioned by Grant was another resolution to reinforce Jessop's proposal of the Boarding School. A conclusion had also been reached in Jessop's mind as to where the first of these Boarding Schools should be located. Kamloops, he thought, would be the ideal spot.

From Kamloops Jessop continued by horseback to Grande Prairie and on to the Okanagan Valley, taking an informal census of the school age population but finding no other schools in operation.

He was back at Yale on October 4 inspecting the school there which was taught by Mr. John Pleace. There were sixteen children making satisfactory progress in their studies in a school house which was in good repair and fairly well equipped. From Yale Jessop made the remaining distance down the Fraser to New Westminster by canoe, stopping off at each settlement where there was a school.[19]

At Hope he found Mrs. Lethbridge teaching nine children. "Reading and Spelling, tolerably good; arithmetic, geography and grammar, just commenced. School well regulated. Children neat and orderly — most half castes. For some time past, the school has been held at the residence of Mrs. Dewdney; the Trustees, however, are about fitting up a room elsewhere."[20] At Chilliwack he found six pupils being taught by Mr. J. McDonald. "School house new and comfortable, but without maps or blackboards; it is about to be removed to a more convenient site, near Chilliwack River, after which the attendance will, probably, be doubled." At the farming community of Sumass the eleven children being taught by Mr. Peers acquitted themselves very creditably. A new school house was in the course of erection there.

Before returning to Victoria Jessop held public meetings in Langley,

Granville and Moodyville resulting in more resolutions supporting the Boarding School proposal.

On October 13 the Victoria *Colonist* announced his return and the results of his survey of the Province's schools:[21]

> John Jessop, Esq., Superintendent of Education, arrived by the steamer *Enterprise* yesterday. Mr. Jessop, during a tour of six weeks on the mainland, has travelled 1,500 miles visiting 9 schools and addressed 12 public meetings. At each of these meetings resolutions were unanimously passed in favour of establishing one or more central boarding schools to meet the wants of the interior. Mr. Jessop found beyond the Cascade Range 407 children, 280 of whom are of school age. Everywhere he found a deep interest manifested in education and a definite conviction that the central boarding school plan is the only one that will meet the needs of the country. Mr. Jessop returns in good health and favourably impressed with the general condition and prospects of the country.

FOOTNOTES

[1] An Act Respecting Public Schools, 1872, Section 8.

[2] Jessop, John, Diary, 1872, June 12, B.C. Archives.

[3] *Ibid.*, June 13, 1872.

[4] Waites, K. A., *The First Fifty Years, 1890-1940. Vancouver High Schools,* Vancouver School Board, 1940, p. 13.

[5] Hamilton, Bea, *Salt Spring Island,* Vancouver, Mitchell Press, 1969, pp. 23, 24.

[6] Jessop, J., First Annual Report on the Public Schools in the Province of British Columbia, 1872, p. 5.

[7] Jessop, J., Diary, 1872, June 29, B.C. Archives.

[8] Grant, George M., *Ocean to Ocean, Sandford Fleming's Expedition Through Canada in 1872,* Toronto, Belford Bros., 1877, pp. 333, 334.

[9] Johnson, Patricia M., *A Short History of Nanaimo,* Nanaimo, Evergreen Press, 1958, p. 38.

[10] Jessop, First Annual Report, p. 6.

[11] *Colonist,* August 30, 1872, p. 3.

[12] West, Willie J. "Staging and Stage Hold-Ups in the Cariboo" *B.C. Historical Quarterly,* Vol. XII. No. 3, July 1948, p. 198.

[16] Jessop, J., Supplementary Report, 1872, p. 35.

[14] Jessop, J., First Annual Report, 1872, p. 7.

[15] *Cariboo Sentinel,* Sept. 14, 1872, p. 3.

[16] Jessop. J., Supplementary Report, 1872. p. 35.

[17] Balf, Mary, "Cache Creek School was Interior's First", *Kamloops Daily Sentinel,* April 27, 1968, p. 3.

[18] Grant, George M., *op. cit.,* p. 293.

[19] *Colonist,* October 13, 1872, p. 3.

[20] Jessop, J., Supplementary Report, 1872, p. 36.

[21] *Colonist,* October 13, 1872, p. 3.

CHAPTER NINE

The Cache Creek Experiment

"The question as to how the educational wants of the interior of this Province are to be supplied, is one that I approach under a deep sense of the responsibility involved in attempting to deal with it." Jessop had been wrestling with this problem for several months and was now presenting his proposals in the Supplementary Report he had promised the Government. The four hundred children of the Interior, he pointed out, "are living from two or three to twenty-five or thirty miles apart. They are therefore, so isolated as to render it almost impracticable to get more than six or ten together at any one point. It is obvious that *all* those children cannot reach school in the ordinary way, and to meet the difficulty, a general Boarding School, or system of Boarding Schools, is proposed."[1]

This and other arguments he advanced which seemed incontrovertible. It would cost the Government far less to provide a system of centralized Boarding Schools than to dot the Interior with little one-room school houses with perhaps no more than half-a-dozen pupils on their rolls.

He presented two plans to the Government for consideration. First: that about nine small boarding schools be built in the Interior each to accommodate no more than fifty children. These would be located at several strategic points in the Cariboo, Thompson and Okanagan regions. Should this scheme be preferred, he recommended starting with two schools, one at Kamloops and the other at Soda Creek which then was the southern terminus for the paddle-wheelers on the Upper Fraser. His alternate proposal was "to erect at some point, say near Cache Creek, a large Central Boarding School, or two, male and female," to accommodate one hundred pupils.

Parents would be expected to contribute "a reasonable sum monthly for their children's board, in money, cattle or farm produce; and keep them comfortably and respectably clothed and properly supplied with bedding, etc." He suggested twelve dollars per month as almost, but not quite, covering the cost of board, but indigent children should be boarded free. Most of these, he estimated, would be "half-breeds who, deserted by their white fathers, have gone with their Indian mothers to the rancheries. Those children, as well as others, will be just what education or the want of it may make them." Educating such children would mold them into useful members of society, neglect might turn them to crime.

At this point the Boarding School proposal became a political prize to be fought over by local politicians. Jessop had originally thought of Kamloops as the most favourable location if there were to be only one. The Board of Education in March 1873 passed a motion that "if there is to be a Boarding School the Government should request the opinion of the Board as to its location" and the Board suggested Kamloops.[2] Much to their chagrin, a month later they learned that the Government had decided to build it at Cache Creek.[3]

Why Cache Creek? There was no town or even village there at that time. Cache Creek was a small stream flowing into the Bonaparte River about six miles north of Ashcroft. It was a pleasant little oasis of greenery amid the vast brown hills of the dry belt — a country as arid as North Africa. The supporters of Cache Creek as the site for the school could argue, however, that it was a central point in the Interior road system because here the Kamloops wagon road branched off to the east while the main road continued north to the Cariboo.

The real reason for the choice, however, was political. The proprietor of Cache Creek's Dominion Ranch was Charles A. Semlin, a member of the Provincial Legislature, an Ontarian and former teacher, who had come to British Columbia in 1862 in search of gold. Not finding it, he had become the manager of the Cornwall Ranch near Ashcroft and had also operated the Bonaparte House, a road-house at Cache Creek. He had been appointed the first post-master of Cache Creek when that spot achieved the dignity of a post-office. From the profits and sale of the Bonaparte House, he acquired the Dominion Ranch of twelve thousand acres and some fifteen hundred head of cattle — one of the great ranches of the Interior. Politically Semlin was a man to be reckoned with. (He eventually became premier of the province.) He and his friends understandably wanted the school at Cache Creek and his influence with the Government decided the issue.[4]

The Department of Lands and Works arranged for the erection of a building in 1873 and D. W. Withrow of New Westminster was given the contract to build it. Ten acres at the confluence of the Bonaparte and Cache Creek were "donated" by James Campbell and Philip Parke with the stipulation that this land be used only for school purposes but no written title to the land was ever transferred to the Government.[5]

The Boarding School was to be a different type of public school, under different control, management and financing from the other schools of the provincial system. New legislation was therefore necessary and in the 1874 session Semlin introduced an Act Respecting the Management of Public Boarding Schools which received legislative approval. Under this act the Boarding School was to have its own trustees but these were not to be elected in the usual fashion but rather appointed by the Government. The new board consisted of Senator C. F. Cornwall (Semlin's former employer), Charles Semlin, James Campbell (the former owner of the Dominion Ranch) and Philip Parke (a former partner of Semlin in Bonaparte House). The enterprise had taken on the appearance of a local business venture and over the next few years the school's business contributed considerable sums into the coffers of these Cache Creek promoters.

In 1874 Jessop made a spring tour into the Interior, stopping at Cache Creek on his way up in May to confer with Semlin and to see to the freighting of furniture and supplies to the school so that all might be ready for the official opening in June.[6]

The two key persons who would take charge of this experimental institution were J. T. Jones, the principal and his wife, the matron, appointed at salaries of $75 and $50 a month respectively. Little is known about the Jones couple other than that they were both English and Mr. Jones held a first class certificate.

The opening of the first Provincial Boarding School took place on June 2. The thirty residents of the district with their families and the eighteen pupils who had gathered for the grand occasion saw a large frame building of two stories. Well proportioned, with porches running the length of the building on both floors, it had a certain simple "colonial" dignity standing stark in its valley ringed by the bare brown hills.

The chairman on the occasion was Charles Semlin, who, after explaining the purpose and design of the school, called on the Super-intendent to address the meeting. John Jessop

observed that he had looked forward to this day with very great pleasure, not unmixed with anxiety; a new era in the education of the country was now commenced. Speaking of the history of the establishment, he gave the credit of being the originator of the movement to the Rev. J. B. Good, who, three years ago, suggested the establishment of some such system and the more he thought upon the matter the more earnestly he was impressed with the fact that this system was not only absolutely necessary, but also, he believed the only one suited to the peculiar wants of this portion of the country . . . He had just gone over an area of upwards to ten thousand square miles, and at no point was it possible to establish a day school. He found three or four children here; twenty or thirty miles away four or five others and so on; and to illustrate the movable nature as well as sparse character of the population, he instanced Clinton, where a schoolhouse was built last year at a cost of $800, and was now closed in consequence of the removal of two families from the place.

Many, he said, looked with great doubt upon the experiment and predicted failure; but each day added to his conviction that it was going to be a great success; so much so that next year another would be required for another district, and the following year another.[7]

For the first year Jessop rode high on a pink cloud of optimism. Others might have doubts about the experiment but not he. In his Third Annual Report in September 1874 he wrote that "the success of the boarding school scheme being assured, I feel no hesitation in strongly recommending that a sum of money be put down in the Estimates of next year for the erection of another building of the same class as the one at Cache Creek, somewhere on the wagon road within a few miles of Soda Creek".[8]

By 1875 the attendance at the school had risen from the initial eighteen pupils to thirty-nine and a $5000 addition to the school was authorized. The building was extended southward toward Cache Creek and the upper storey was divided into two dormitories, for boys and girls. In the spring Jessop made his annual visit to Cache Creek, meeting with the trustees to discuss the new construction and holding a public examination of the school. The entry in his diary was entirely complimentary to the school, its pupils and its administration:

Children neat, orderly and attentive to studies — making good improvement in behaviour and manners. They are seemingly quite happy and contented. Everything well systematized — well pleased with examination — all arrangements in school, kitchen, dining-room and dormitories of most satisfactory description —

The Principal is active and energetic. He has not only to look after the school but to attend to nearly all the multifarious business matters pertaining to the establishment — Mrs. Jones is admirably adapted for the onerous position of matron — Her quiet motherly demeanor and constant attention to the wants of the children are deserving of the greatest possible commendation — Mrs. Jones also is a great help in the school, taking as she does all the duties of assistant. If desirous of finding fault, it would be difficult for an unprejudiced person to do so in and around the Cache Creek Boarding School.[9]

Before leaving, Jessop requested the principal to prepare and mail to him a special report on his school in time for this to be included in the Superintendent's annual report. However, by the time Jessop had to write his report there was still no news from Jones. Jessop was beginning to have his doubts about the reliability of the principal. "No returns having come to hand from this establishment (Cache Creek), I have not the data for such a report as its importance demands . . . The only excuse received from the principal for the non-fulfilment of this duty is that 'harvest and politics must be held answerable for the delay of our returns, &c.'"[10]

Early in 1876 evident signs of mismanagement of the school began to appear. The trustees were concerned over the fraternization of boys and girls, requiring separation of the sexes at meal time. Fees were haphazardly collected and unpaid debts for supplies accumulated. Strange goings-on must have prompted the trustees to pass the resolution that "The Board deem it advisable that no one except pupils be boarded at the school".[11]

Complaints and rumors reached Victoria and a Select Committee of the Legislature was struck to report on the Cache Creek situation. Jessop's Board of Education in March instructed him "to investigate certain charges made against Mr. Jones . . . as soon as possible". This he proposed to do on his spring tour.[12]

When the Select Committee made its report it recommended an end to the coeducational policy of the boarding school, suggesting that separate boys' and girls' schools be established. It objected to the practice of having pupils do the menial chores around the establishment and to the building being used for balls and political meetings. They recommended that the appointment and dismissal of teachers be vested in the cabinet, and "that a Deputy Superintendent be appointed for and reside on the Mainland at some central point; the Provincial

Secretary to act as Superintendent on the Island".[13] This was, of course, a clear affront to Jessop. It would have eliminated his office. Jessop had his enemies in high places. If the Boarding School policy were to fail, Jessop himself would be vulnerable. In May an amended and consolidated school act created the post of Deputy Superintendent of Education. The legislature disregarded the recommendation that the Provincial Secretary assume the Superintendency on the Island and confirmed Jessop in his position.

In the meantime Principal Jones had resigned and the Board replaced him with Archibald Irwin, a Canadian teaching in the Nicola Valley. Mrs. Irwin was appointed matron.

Jessop visited Cache Creek in June, by which time the Irwins had taken charge of the school. He returned to submit to the Provincial Secretary a startling exposé of conditions in the school under Jones. The letter was included in his Fifth Annual Report and subsequently touched off a great deal of unfavorable publicity in the newspapers.[14] Jessop found that the liabilities of the school amounted to $2200 with creditors "impatiently clamoring for settlement".

> The building, which was so well provided with every requisite two years ago, is now almost destitute of kitchen and dining room furniture. The great amount of breakage of crockery, lamps, lamp chimneys, table forks &c, &c, &c, said to have taken place must have been the result of carelessness on the part of the authorities in charge. Two first class cooking stoves, of the largest size, and some of the box stoves, are much damaged and nearly burnt out. One of the doors is broken off its hinges, and the panels of another are split. Since the completion of the addition to the building, last autumn, several panes of glass have been broken. The entire edifice has therefore a dilapidated and neglected appearance.

Attendance had fallen from 44 in June 1875 to 15 a year later. Jessop laid the blame largely on the board for its lack of interest and on the "neglect of the Secretary-Treasurer, or his inability", to attend to the school's business. In consequence the late teacher had been saddled with these duties in addition to his own. He too had been neglectful of his responsibilities. "It is very evident that Mr. Jones had too much private business on his hands which prevented him from doing justice to the school. A great deal of time seems to have been bestowed upon teaming, trading, &c, &c that should have been devoted to school work."

Jessop made a number of recommendations to restore the school's physical condition, pay off its debts, to keep the sexes separate and avoid future difficulties. He advocated the appointment of "a conscientous first class teacher, well acquainted with bookkeeping and possessing good business habits" as a Deputy Superintendent in the Interior. Jessop no doubt hoped that this would be the end of the matter and that the school could get back to normal under a new principal and matron, but alas, this was not to be!

In the summer the appointment to the post of Deputy Superintendent was made. It went to Robert M. Clemitson, a Victoria teacher. He was to reside at Cache Creek, supervise that establishment and inspect the Interior schools.

In a letter to Jessop in October 1876 Clemitson alluded to "rumours of immorality as have obtained currency in the past" but assured him that "the sexes, as far as the internal arrangements of the establishment are concerned, are practically separated now by the recent addition to the building, which has secured distinct entrances to the dormitories".[15] However, the following March he revealed in another letter to Jessop that the rumors of immorality had a very definite basis in fact and that the school now had a first-rate scandal on its hands, the details of which had titillated the ears of gossips from Boston Bar to Barkerville. A proportion of the pupils at Cache Creek were hardly children but young men and women, well endowed with the usual animal spirits which had sought release from the confinement of a boarding school. During the year he had discovered that some of the girls had been frequenting the boys' dormitory at night by the simple expedient of opening the door in the partition between the two dormitories by unbolting it on the girls' side! "I never for a moment supposed," wrote the shocked principal Irwin, "that the girls would be the aggressors."[16] The façade of Victorian respectability was shattered; Jessop groaned; the Government was embarrassed; the Principal resigned; the Boarding School was again in jeopardy — and newspapers were delighted. Clemitson's letter was reprinted in the *Colonist* and a spate of correspondence followed.[17] Rumors circulated that the school would be changed into a day school or that the coeducational feature would be abandoned.

Clemitson in his letter had suggested that the environmental influences and "the horrible state of social life here" were largely to blame and considered that the trustees were "not the men qualified by social standing, soundness of judgement and thorough discretion to discharge successfully the duties of their position". This criticism, of course, raised the ire of the trustees who presented to Premier A. C. Elliott a memorial staunchly defending their actions, blaming Irwin and Clemitson and appealing to the premier to retain the institution as a coeducational boarding school.

> In reference to the future of the school we are of the opinion that it can be conducted as a mixed school without the occurrences of the past being repeated; and we beg earnestly to impress upon you that, owing to the isolated position of the settlers in this part of the Province, many of the residents will be wholly unable to avail themselves of a day school, and if this institution is closed will be compelled to raise their chidren in ignorance. We therefore earnestly beg that our only means of education be allowed to remain a boarding school.[18]

The Government heeded the trustees' pleas and did not close the school. Soon the press lost interest, and "the Cache Creek Scandal" became a thing of the past. In the meantime Thomas Leduc, an Ontarian who had been teaching at Lillooet, replaced Irwin as principal and Mrs. Augustus Schubert became the matron. The Provincial Board of Education laid down new regulations for the school which admitted girls of all ages but boys only to the age of ten. Fees had now to be paid in advance and were to include the pupil's laundry.[19] Clemitson continued as Deputy Superintendent and inspected the Interior schools.

Under the management of Leduc and Mrs. Schubert the school won new respectability and the enrolment recovered. Leduc seems to have been a very good teacher. When Jessop next inspected the school he noted a marked improvement in the classes. "The continuous control and superintendence of the teacher, combining steady regard to home work with the special duties of the school-room, have borne fruit in the rapid progress of many of the scholars . . . The deportment of the pupils in the school-room and their behaviour while entering and leaving, were admirable, promptness, quietness and order characterizing all their movements. The cleanly and healthy appearance of the children was very pleasing and the genuine interest with which they went through their recitations augured well for future progress."[20]

Much of the credit for the improved appearance and behavior of the children was probably due to the motherly care of Mrs. Schubert, a highly respected pioneer of the Interior. Catherine Schubert had accompanied her husband, Augustus, in a party of "Overlanders" across the plains and mountains and down the North Thompson in 1862, arriving at Fort Kamloops just in time to give birth there to the first white child born in Kamloops.[21] Mrs. Schubert's youngest daughter, Catherine, was a pupil at Cache Creek and in later years set down her recollections of life in the school:[22]

> The pupils came from as far away as New Westminster, Nicola Valley, Kamloops, Lillooet, Cariboo, Clinton, and Hat Creek. Many families living on farms around Cache Creek preferred their children to board at the school. It really was a splendid training as well as an education for those boys and girls.
>
> When I look back on my stay at that school, I think it was marvellous how smoothly it was run. No disturbances of any kind, and all the girls loved by my mother.
>
> Our entertainment was very simple. We had music and every evening we marched into the large dining room and sang. Miss Lawrence was the pianist and now, as I think of it, I consider that she had a great deal of patience. Some of us would be out of tune and time, but we enjoyed it all.
>
> Every Saturday we went hill-climbing, for the eminences were really hills, not mountains. Sunday service was held in the schoolroom, attended by both boys and girls and a school teacher. We had school lessons in the very large classroom, boys and girls together; but playgrounds and living quarters were separate. The schoolmaster had control of the boys.
>
> We had regular hours for everything — music, study, getting up, meals and going to bed. After all the girls had gathered in the dormitory, mother would wait till we were ready for bed and knelt to say prayers. All the beds were in white, some single, some larger. I must admit that I sometimes looked around, and it was quite a nice sight to see the girls all kneeling in their white nightdresses. Then mother would see that we were all comfortable and say good-night. I have never forgotten that part of our life; it made a great impression on me.

Life flowed pleasantly and uneventfully at Cache Creek Boarding School for a dozen years longer. The quality of the instruction and management left little to be desired but throughout the 1880's the enrolment gradually declined.

In 1883 the school lost both Thomas Leduc and Mrs. Schubert who, with her children, went to Enderby to join her husband on a farm there and Leduc went with them to take up land in the same region. Robert Clemitson left the Deputy Superintendency in 1880 to farm at Grande Prairie but returned to take over the principalship from Leduc. He retired in 1887 and Joseph Irwin, a brother of the former principal, Archibald Irwin, carried on until 1890. Then with only a dozen pupils in attendance, the school finally closed its doors.[23]

By this time the once meager centers of population in the Interior had increased through immigration to the point where each could support a local school and a central boarding establishment was no longer needed. When nearby Ashcroft opened its own school in 1889 it was evident that Cache Creek had outlived its usefulness.[24]

For many years after it had ceased to function as a school the old frame building stood beside the chuckling creek, wind-weathered and sun-tanned to the colour of the surrounding hills — a ghostly reminder of the childhood memories of many pioneers of the Interior.

FOOTNOTES

[1] Jessop, J., Supplementary Report for 1872, p. 38. For much of the material in this chapter I am indebted to the M.A. thesis of John Calam, "An Historical Survey of Boarding Schools and Public School Dormitories in Canada", University of British Columbia, 1962, ch. IV.

[2] Minutes of the Board of Education, March 12, 1873, p. 50, B.C. Archives.

[3] *Ibid.,* April 15, 1873, p. 52.

[4] Jackman, S. W., *Portraits of the Premiers,* Sidney, Gray's Publishing Ltd., 1969, pp. 112, 113. Semlin became premier of British Columbia in 1898.

[5] *Colonist,* April 12, 1876, p. 3.

[6] Jessop, John, Diary, May 12, 1874, B.C. Archives.

[7] *The Daily Standard,* Victoria, June 8, 1874, p. 3.

[8] Third Annual Report of the Superintendent of Education, Sept. 1874, p. 23.

[9] Jessop, John, Diary, May 31, 1875, B.C. Archives.

[10] Fourth Annual Report of the Superintendent of Education, 1874-75, p. 97.

[11] Calam, *op. cit.,* p. 81.

[12] Minutes of the Board of Education, March 14, 1876, B.C. Archives.

[13] Report of the Select Committee on Public Schools. Sessional Papers of British Columbia, 1876, p. 588.

[14] Fifth Annual Report of the Superintendent of Education, 1875-76, pp. 95-97.

[15] *Ibid.,* p. 99.

[16] Calam, *op. cit.,* p. 86.

[17] *Colonist,* April 15, 1877, p. 2.

[18] Memorial of Messrs. Parke, Sanford, Semlin and Barnes to Hon. A.C. Elliott, Sessional Papers of British Columbia, 1878, pp. 440, 441.

[19] Sessional Papers of British Columbia, 1878, p. 442.

[20] Sixth Annual Report of the Superintendent of Education, 1876-77, p. 24.

[21] Fort Kamloops Journal, Oct. 15, 1862. This daughter of Mrs. Schubert was Rose (Mrs. Henry Swanson of Armstrong).

[22] Fraser, Mrs. H. A., "Reminiscences of the Old Days", *Okanagan Historical Society Report of 1950,* pp. 129-133. Mrs. Schubert's story is also told in *Journey Fantastic* by Vicky Metcalfe (Toronto, Ryerson, 1970).

[23] Calam, *op. cit.,* p. 89.

[24] Balf, *op. cit.,* p. 3.

CHAPTER TEN

Creating A School System

The founders of our school systems are generally either totally ignored by historians or relegated to the near-oblivion of a footnote or a line or two in a history book. And yet few men have had more influence on the thinking, the culture, the attitudes and mores of generations of our people than those who have designed and established the public school systems. Jessop realized this and knew that his was the unique honor and the attendant responsibility of setting that system on a sound foundation.

His preoccupation with the educational needs of British Columbia's sparsely populated hinterland was but one of the many problems he met in creating a school system for a burgeoning province. During the seven formative years of his incumbency he had to consider the central problem of what should be the social function of the school system within the context of the province's development. He had to recruit teachers, certificate them, train and advise them and see to their welfare. He had to develop a curriculum, inspect the schools and cope, almost single-handedly, with a multitude of administrative details. As each year added more new districts to the system this involved relationships with an increasing number of school boards. He had to advise the Government on school financing and press that Government and the people of the province step by step to achieve the goal of an education for every child.

In Jessop's mind there was never any question as to the model on which his system should, in its general principles, be based. That, of course, was the public school system headed by Egerton Ryerson in Ontario, for which he had been trained and where he had gained his first experience as a schoolmaster. He advanced no claim to originality. In fact he referred with some pride to "that admirable school system upon which ours is founded."[1] Gosnell, a contemporary of Jessop, noted in 1903 that "the present school system of British

Columbia, which has been in operation since 1872 is, in its most salient features, a copy of the Ontario Act of 1846. The immense extent of the province, however, and the sparseness of the population, have rendered it necessary to modify, in many important particulars, the provisions of that Act."[2]

One of Jessop's first official acts, after taking over the office of Superintendent, was to write to Dr. J. George Hodgins, Ryerson's Deputy, asking for "copies of the Chief Superintendent's Reports, the Journal of Education, the new School Act and other Departmental papers which from time to time are issued from your office."[3] It will be recalled that Jessop had been authorized by his Board of Education to purchase all the necessary textbooks from the Toronto publishing firm of Campbell and Son. These were the same books which this company supplied to the Ontario Schools and Jessop managed to get them at the eastern retail prices. They were then resold to the schools with copies provided free to indigent pupils. School equipment and supplies such as maps and blackboards were purchased by the Education Department and presented to the schools that required them. At first there was a wide variety of textbooks in use — hand-me-down readers, geographies and spellers which had once been used by the pupils' parents. Soon the authorized texts replaced these and the resulting uniformity made curricula possible. By 1876 Jessop could report that "all the schools are supplied with maps and terrestrial globes. With one or two exceptions they are all furnished with blackboards. The authorized textbooks are now exclusively used throughout the Province."[4] To provide the necessary stock of books and school supplies Jessop again followed the Ontario model in establishing in 1873 a Book Depository under the Department but by 1877 he reported that "as supplies of school books and stationery can now be procured through the ordinary trade channels as cheaply as from the Education depository, its further continuance might be considered as an uncalled for competition with the Provincial booksellers."[5]

One typical Ontario school custom which Jessop attempted to introduce into British Columbia was that province's curious system of merit cards and prize books. When Ryerson took over the Superintendency in Ontario he was much disturbed by the prevalence of corporal punishment in the schools. It was excessively used not merely to punish flagrant misbehavior but as a constant stimulus to learning. This he felt was inhumane and unnecessary, a brutalizing influence on both pupils and teachers. He proposed to approach the problem of discipline and motivation to learn by the positive means of rewards rather than through the negative method of punishments. His answer was the merit card and prize book system. The Department of Education in Ontario printed thousands of little cards containing a scriptural exhortation to diligence and good conduct and stating that the recipient was entitled to this reward of merit. These were distributed to the teachers who were expected to award them daily to those pupils who had earned such through diligence, punctuality or good conduct. At the end of the term those pupils with sufficient merit cards were to receive a prize book suitably inscribed. The local school board purchased and awarded the prize books but the Department in Ontario provided them at cost prices and added a one hundred percent bonus. The merit cards were furnished to the boards at a small charge. The Ontario teachers complained of the excessive amount of book-keeping which the system required but Ryerson was strongly convinced of its value.

Jessop ordered a sample supply of the Ontario prize books and merit cards and tried, not very successfully, to sell the idea to his own school boards and teachers in his Fourth Annual Report. Rather than have the Department cover the cost of these items he tried to persuade the school boards and teachers to purchase them. In support of the system he quoted at length from Dr. Ryerson's arguments in its favor. The principle behind the system, Ryerson had said, was that "on which Divine Government itself is based, namely, rewarding every one according to his works . . . If the distribution of prizes is decided fairly according to merit there can be no just ground for dissatisfaction; and facilities are now provided and their employment prescribed, with a view to determine the merit of punctuality, of good conduct, of diligence, of proficiency on the part of each pupil during each term of the year — a four-fold motive to exertion and emulation in everything that constitutes a good pupil and a good school . . . The prize book system and especially in connection with that of merit cards has a most salutary influence upon the School discipline, upon both teachers and pupils, besides diffusing a large amount of entertaining and useful reading."[6]

Another feature of the Ontario educational system which Jessop admired and which he sought to introduce to British Columbia was the public library service operated by the Department of Education. When Ryerson introduced the scheme in the 1840's books were expensive and difficult to obtain. The Canadian farmer's chief source of reading matter was the newspaper which he read and passed on to his neighbors. Ryerson, through his Book Depository, purchased and stocked library books and assisted school boards to establish small local libraries, usually in the village school houses. By 1870 Ontario had the remarkable number of 1146 common school libraries operated by school boards and free to pupils, teachers and the general public.[7] Governor General Lord Elgin had praised this library system in 1854 as "the Crown and Glory of the Institutions of the Province."[8]

Might the people of British Columbia support such an excellent system? Jessop perhaps had some doubts in his mind but in his Sixth Annual Report he proposed a public library system on the lines of Ontario's:

> Nearly twenty-five years experience in Ontario has fully proved that school libraries have exercised, and are still exercising, a most beneficial influence upon the minds of the young. They have contributed largely to the high standard of intelligence and moral rectitude for which the present generation in that favoured Province are justly celebrated . . . No better investment of a few hundred dollars of the Provincial revenue could be made than of supplementing, as in Ontario, to the extent of about fifty percent, whatever sums might be contributed by school districts for such a purpose. Settlers in various parts of the Province, whether parents or not, would readily avail themselves of such an offer of securing standard works on science and art, biography and travel, poetry and fiction if fifty percent could be added to their contributions and the books supplied them at Eastern wholesale prices . . . Not only would school libraries exert a healthy influence upon neighborhoods as a whole, but they could not fail to prove a powerful auxiliary in the hands of teachers (who should act as librarians) in lessening irregularity in school attendance and absenteeism, by offering inducements for reading and improving the mind, which would tend to outweigh and counteract temptations to idleness and its numerous train of vices. The subject is presented to the people of British Columbia, in the hope that something may be done in the direction indicated, and that ere long we shall be following in the footsteps of the sister Province in what has proved to be of the greatest possible benefit to thousands of her population.

The proposal failed to stir much enthusiasm among the teachers or trustees and certainly not among members of the Government who at this time favored retrenchment rather than what could be an expensive public service. However, it did illustrate the scope of Jessop's educational plans for the Province and his devotion to the Ontario model.

When Jessop first assumed the Superintendency there were in existence or in the process of formation, only twenty-five school districts, all of which he visited in his first inspectoral tour. Only twelve of these were on the mainland. By 1878, his last year in office, another twenty districts had been added. On Vancouver Island new districts developed near Victoria at Colwood, near Nanaimo at Cedar and at the coal-mining community of Wellington. In the Gulf Islands Burgoyne Bay on Saltspring became a separate district and the Gabriola and Denman Island districts were organized. As settlement spread into the fertile lower Fraser Valley school districts sprang up at Cheam, Maple Ridge, Matsqui, Prairie (Langley Prairie) and at York which was at the head of Sumass Lake.[10] Below New Westminster two new school districts were formed at North Arm (in what is now South Vancouver) and in the area then called Trenant, a farming community on the south bank of the Fraser at its mouth opposite Tilbury Island. This has since become the town of Ladner. In the Interior a school district was created at "Okanagan" in 1874, in the five-mile perimeter north of Mission Creek which is now in the city of Kelowna. Other Interior districts developed in the Nicola Valley, at Cache Creek, Lac La Hache, Stuart Lake and Stanley, a little settlement on July Creek west of the present town of Grand Forks.

In 1872-73 the Province's school districts had an aggregate enrolment of 1028; in 1877-78 this had doubled to 2198.[11]

The relationship that existed between the Department of Education and its school boards in these early days of the Province was scarcely one of partnership in the educational enterprise. The system was highly centralized with power and responsibility almost entirely in the hands of the Provincial Board of Education and its Superintendent. The functions of the local boards were then very much limited as compared with their present responsibilities. They were, however, expected to be the local guardians and informants of the central authority and to cooperate actively in persuading parents to send as many children of school age as possible to school and to send them regularly.

Jessop had his difficulties with the trustees. He complained frequently of their procrastination in submitting necessary returns and information from the districts. The almost complete centralization of authority tended to develop an attitude among trustees that it was the "Government's" school, not theirs and whatever needed to be done for it was the "Government's" responsibility. Jessop expressed his dissatisfaction with this attitude in his Third Annual Report:[12]

> In many districts, a deplorable want of interest is manifested by Trustee Boards and parents in the success and progress of their schools. It is difficult, in some instances, to get their Annual Reports even imperfectly filled up; while the teacher is left entirely to his or her devices, not only in the conduct of the school, but in many things that ought to be looked after by the Trustees. Willingness to cooperate with the Government in keeping the school buildings in repair, or improving them, seems to be diminishing, rather than increasing; so much so, that if a tree in a dangerous position requires to be cut down, a log rolled out of the way, a piece of fencing to be done, or a picket to be nailed up, the school grant must be taxed to do it. I have often been met with the reply, when suggesting the propriety of those interested, or who ought to be interested in the success of public schools, doing something in aid of preparing a lot for the erection of a school house, putting up a wood shed, or making a piece of fencing, 'Oh, the Government should pay for everything, they are well able to do it.' People seem to forget that, in other Provinces and Countries, there is such a thing as direct and even local taxation for educational purposes, and that the manifestation of such a spirit may, sooner or later, induce the Government and Legislature to consider the advisability of levying such a tax; not only for increasing the revenue of the Province, but to give trustees, parents and others a direct interest in curtailing expenditure and economizing school funds.

In 1873 a dispute arose between Jessop and the Victoria school board which was aired in the local press.[13] Jessop had suggested to this board that an enrolment of 156 in the Victoria Boys' School and 190 in the Girls' School, each with two teachers, was excessive overcrowding and advised the trustees to reduce this by opening a third school and hiring two additional teachers. When the Victoria *Standard* publicized the overcrowding this set off an exchange of letters in the press between the school board and Jessop. The trustees accused the Superintendent of being laggard in presenting their financial needs to the

Government and Jessop blamed them for misrepresenting the issue and neglecting to take action on the problem of overcrowding.

Jessop had a marked propensity for presenting his side of a dispute in the press — possibly arising from his earlier association with newspaper work. Such action would today be regarded as unpardonable conduct for a civil servant, but in those days the mute apolitical decorum of the senior civil servant had not yet been established as a parliamentary tradition. Ryerson, Jessop's counterpart in Ontario, continually resorted to the press to air his side of a controversy. Like Ryerson, Jessop could never allow personal criticism to stand unrefuted. This may have set the record straight but oftentimes it made more enemies than friends.

Two years later, he was involved in another press duel with the Nanaimo board. The trustees had called for tenders for some repairs to their school. When their choice of tender was rejected by Jessop and his Board of Education as being too high, Jessop called for tenders in the Victoria papers. This raised the hackles of the Nanaimo board which voiced its objection in the Nanaimo *Free Press*. This letter in turn was reprinted in the Victoria *Colonist*.[14] Jessop replied in a very lengthy letter in the Victoria paper in which he revealed that only one tender had been received by the Nanaimo board and that from the board's secretary-treasurer! "I enquired of another carpenter doing business in Nanaimo," wrote Jessop, "why he did not compete for the work, when he replied that 'it was no use for him or any one else to tender while the Secretary-Treasurer was allowed to do so, as he had an undue advantage over all others; and that he would not tender for any work under such circumstances'."[15] Political life was obviously less sophisticated in those days and political chicanery more openly accepted as part of the natural order of public life.

However, with most boards Jessop was on the best of terms. Trustees usually were men of little formal education who looked up to the Superintendent as the source from which all educational blessings must flow. One simple missive from a school board secretary might serve to illustrate:[16]

Burgoyne Bay March 16 1878.

Mr. Jessop
    Sir the school children is all well of the whooping cough please send us up a teacher as soon as possible
Yours truly
John Maxwell

Jessop's first tour of inspection had brought to light a woeful lack of suitable school buildings. Only eight schools then were public property. In the other districts schools were held wherever accommodation was available by donation or by rental. Jessop and his Department launched a building programme which by 1874 had increased the number of publicly-owned school houses to twenty-eight but even then, as he reported, "four buildings are still rented for school purposes, at a monthly rental of $34, namely, one in Victoria at $20 per month, one in Esquimalt at $4, one in Hope at $5, and one in Lillooet at $5. Two Courthouses are occupied as school rooms — one at North Cowichan, and the other in Lytton. The school house in Granville is the property of the Hastings Mill Company, but is occupied rent free."[17]

Almost all these school buildings were simple, unpretentious one-room wooden school houses. In 1875 Jessop had the satisfaction of seeing the Province's first large substantial brick school house erected in Victoria. With inordinate pride he described it as it rose to completion on the school reserve at the head of Yates and View Streets:

This edifice is in the Italian style of architecture, on a stone foundation, and built of well-burnt local red brick, relieved by sandstone dressings around the windows and outside doors. It consists of two lofty storeys, in addition to which there is a large and well-lighted room in the mansard roof. The ground floor will be occupied by the boys' department, with an entrance from the east, entirely separate from that of the girls, who will use the front or western door, and ascend a fine staircase to the second flat. On each floor, the main school rooms are rather more than 70 feet by 40 feet, having a floor space of 3000 superficial feet. These rooms have ample accommodation for 300 children. The desks and settees are double, and of most approved description, with revolving seats; passages between each row giving the teachers easy access to every pupil. One large school room on each floor was considered preferable to increasing the size or number of gallery rooms; as by such a plan the entire department can be seated for general purposes, such as opening and closing exercises, writing, singing, distribution of prizes, addresses, etc., etc. . . . the large rooms will be heated by means of hot air stoves, while the smaller ones have open fire-places protected by fire guards. In addition to every window having casements to open, there are ventilating flues to each department. Commodious hat

114

and cloak rooms, lavatories, etc., are provided for; an arrangement is also made for a supply of pure water.[18]

The *Colonist* reporter noted that in the main room a blackboard ran "all around the room in place of wainscotting thereby affording ample space for the demonstration of problems in arithmetic, algebra, etc." The arrangement on each floor for a large open area with smaller rooms off it immediately suggests to the modern teacher the "open area school" which has been very much in vogue with school authorities in the 1960's and '70's.

It was one of the grandest buildings in Victoria, the last word in school architecture and probably the most attractive school building on the whole Pacific coast. "True, some of the school edifices in San Francisco are more pretentious in appearance; but none of them have such extensive and beautiful grounds, or such magnificent views of city, country, and surrounding waters."

The curriculum or course of studies of a provincial school system to-day is set out in considerable detail in one or more books prepared and published and placed in the hands of teachers by the Department of Education. In Jessop's time, there was no such publication. The curriculum was essentially the list of authorized text books. Some idea of the subjects which were considered more worthy of emphasis than others may be assumed from the regulations governing the examinations of teachers for certification.[19] Described as "ordinary subjects, more or less essential" were spelling, reading, writing, composition, grammar, arithmetic, book-keeping, geography and history. "Extraordinary subjects less or more non-essential" were "mathematics for each branch", Latin, French, drawing and music.

Reading was taught from the Canadian Readers, a graded series consisting of five books plus an "Advanced Reader". Spelling was taught from the *Canadian Spelling Book*. The other authorized texts included Lennie's *Grammar*, J. G. Hodgson's *Easy Lessons in Geography*, Campbell's *Modern Geography and Atlas*, Smith and McMurchy's *Elementary* and *Advanced Arithmetics*, Collier's *Outlines of General History, British Empire*, and *British History*, Colenso's *Algebra*, Young's *Euclid* and Rulton and Eastman's *Book-keeping*.[20] In addition to these there were other subjects taught apparently without authorized texts, i.e., "natural philosophy", vocal music, linear drawing, writing and dictation. It may seem strange that algebra, geometry and book-keeping had a place in an elementary school curriculum but it was not unusual in eastern Canada for some teachers, who were capable of teaching certain high school subjects, to offer them in rural schools in what were called "continuation classes" or "Fifth Book classes." In British Columbia only in a few schools, in the larger centers, Victoria, New Westminster and Nanaimo, were teachers offering higher mathematics.

There seemed to be some confusion in the minds of the Board of Education as to the academic respectability of certain branches of the fine arts. In the Superintendent's absence in 1872 the Board directed the principal of the Victoria Girls' School to discontinue the teaching of instrumental music and in 1875 they incurred the wrath of Terpsichore by informing the Victoria school board that it could not carry on an after-hours dancing class in the same Broughton Street Girls School.[21] This, of course, may have resulted from objections by certain religious groups to dancing or it may merely have reflected a dislike, not unknown to-day, to "frills" in education.

It would seem that Jessop did not share these views. In his Second Annual Report he made a strong plea for teachers to try teaching vocal music. "This branch of instruction", he wrote, "is not so generally taught in our schools as it ought to be. It should be considered an essential, instead of an unimportant non-essential . . . Probably nine out of ten persons of both sexes will find far more use for, and derive greater benefit from, a fair knowledge of this subject than from mathematics beyond the simple rules of arithmetic."[22] A year later he was pleased to see it being well taught in the Victoria school.[23] He occasionally went back to the Victoria school to give a vocal music lesson himself.

In his Fourth Annual Report Jessop again took up his pen in defense of the arts — this time of drawing. "In this progressive age, free hand or linear drawing is every day becoming more and more necessary in almost every position in life . . . The object to be aimed at, is not so much to enable boys and girls to 'make pretty pictures' as to train them to construct a passably good outline of any figure that they may see, or the idea of which may be presented to their minds." He quoted Henry Barnard, the first United States Commissioner of Education on the subject — "Drawing should be taught in every grade of our Public Schools. The first instinct or inclination of the child is to handle the pencil and draw something. "

In the earliest pioneer schools in Canada there had been no classification of pupils by "grades" or "divisions". There was, in fact, no classification at all. Children were individually assigned pages to be read and "learned", i.e., committed to memory, and then in turn the teacher heard and corrected these "recitations". Under such a system no "grading" was necessary. There was some grouping of children according to subjects, i.e., those learning to write (which generally followed some competence in reading and spelling), those studying arithmetic, a few studying geography or history or in rare cases the classics. The authorization of a graded series of Readers in Jessop's time introduced the element of homogeneous grouping according to the stage of progress in reading. A child might then be said to be in the "Second Reader" or "Second Book" class. This was really the beginning of what later became the eight-grade system of the elementary school. In the 1870's Jessop and others were trying to get away from the individual recitation system into some homogeneous class organization. One of the duties of teachers as prescribed by the Board of Education was "to classify the pupils according to their respective abilities."[24]

One of the obstacles to this was the Victorian reluctance to have boys and girls, except in their early years, taught together. Coeducation, they feared, might coarsen their daughters. If, however, boys and girls could be taught together, grading would be easier to arrange and the groups could be large enough for each to employ a separate teacher. Financially, of course, there would be savings through coeducation as fewer teachers would be required. A rural school district might have twenty-five boys and girls of school age. These could all be taught by one teacher if coeducation were the rule — and this fact accounted for the prevalence of mixed classes in all the country schools. It was in the cities that the issue arose.

The School Act of 1872 had empowered the Board of Education to establish separate girls' schools where they might deem it expedient,[25] and in that same year the Board had agreed to do this in the case of the Victoria district.[26] When the new Victoria School was erected, although girls and boys were taught in the same building they were separated physically and administratively into Boys' and Girls' Departments. The playgrounds also were separated by a high board fence. As the boys had a large playing field to themselves, "there can be no excuse", in the eyes of the *Colonist*, "for any of the young gentlemen interfering with the girls except from downright love of mischief."[27] Here and in Nanaimo and New Westminster the local boards had preferred to have their boys and girls taught separately.

Jessop argued against this separation of the sexes in school, both from the financial angle and on the basis of what he called "teaching power", i.e., the advantage of grouping children together for a lesson to save instructional time:[28]

> Keeping the sexes exclusively in separate departments, necessitates two classes in each branch of study throughout the entire school curriculum; whereas, if the two classes — one of boys and the other of girls — be combined for tuition, the gain in teaching power would be nearly doubled. Under the graded system, every class would have a great deal more time for each study, or several studies might be introduced that must inevitably be excluded so long as the sexes are taught separately from each other. It is a well-known and universally conceded fact, that two teachers in a graded school can produce more satisfactory results, with less work, than three can possibly do in one that is not graded.

Jessop refused to concede that girls would become less refined in a coeducational atmosphere:

> The main plea, in fact the only one with a shadow of plausibility, is that the sexes should be educated apart, in order that the girls may grow up with that delicacy and refinement of feeling, that softness and innate modesty so desirable, and so much to be admired in young women. That this result would be interfered with by the coeducation of the sexes, is entirely a mistaken idea . . . This want of confidence in the ability of girls to take care of themselves on the part of parents, and the imperative injunctions laid upon them to 'keep out of the way' of the opposite sex, do more to defeat the very object they wish to attain than all other causes combined. In the prurient desire of such parties to avoid an evil almost entirely imaginary, the great benefits resulting from educating boys and girls together by the healthy and vigorous spirit of emulation, which is thus excited and kept up, are entirely overlooked. They forget that the boisterousness of their sons is being constantly moderated; that the rougher asperities of boyish nature are undergoing a toning-down process; and that the inherent traits of gallantry, affability, and desire to please are fostered by daily association with the softer sex in the public school.

118

Jessop approached his responsibilities in public education with all the missionary zeal of the Methodist. It was part of the Methodist creed to believe in the perfectability of man and in universal education as the means toward that end. The central ideal which Jessop pursued throughout his professional career was quite simple — to achieve a good public school system, to make it free to all, and finally to ensure that all parents sent their children to school to receive its blessings. The Public School Act of 1872 had provided free schooling but had not added the element of compulsion. Many parents in those days, had little desire to see their children educated and even among those pupils who were enrolled in schools irregular attendance slowed their progress and irritated the teachers. In 1872-73 the attendance record of the 1028 children who were registered in schools was only 56%. Jessop and his Board were engaged in a perpetual struggle to achieve compulsory schooling and to improve the attendance factor. They succeeded in 1873 in having the school act amended to permit trustees to make by-laws which would require parents to send children aged seven to fourteen to school.

Jessop soon discovered that boards were exceedingly reluctant to pass such by-laws or to enforce them. In 1874 he observed:

No progress whatever has been made during the past year by Trustee Boards in the enforcement of the compulsory clauses of the School Amendment Act. I am not able to report the enactment of a single additional By-law. Of the two only that have been passed, namely Comox and Sooke, one, at least, seems to be inoperative; for, with twenty-three children whose names appear on the District Register as having attended school some portion of the year, the average is less than seven . . . There is no power vested anywhere to oblige Trustees to comply with the requirements of the law. Even if this power did exist, the attempt to exercise it must prove abortive as no one would then be found willing to undertake the duties of trustee.[29]

The Board then turned from the trustees as the enforcing agents to the teachers. The Rules and Regulations of 1874 made the teacher's salary dependent upon the level of attendance. An average attendance of forty to fifty merited the highest salary (eighty dollars). This scale decreased to the minimum level of fifty dollars for an average attendance of only ten to twenty. This may have forced teachers to make every effort to recruit pupils but it was most unfair to the rural teacher.

Another amendment to the School Act in 1876 required that every child aged seven to twelve inclusive "shall attend some school or be otherwise educated for six months in every year." It further stated that it would be the duty of the trustees or of the Superintendent to lodge a complaint with a magistrate against any parent neglecting to send a school-age child to school. Fines were to be levied on conviction. A year later Jessop noticed a gratifying improvement in the attendance figures but in fact it required much longer than Jessop's term of office and much further development of settlement and road-building before school attendance figures would indicate that every school-age child was receiving an education.

Financially the Education Department seemed to be in a very sound position, in spite of the fact that all costs of education were charged directly to the Province's general revenues. There was as yet no local taxation for school purposes. The costs of education inevitably rose in Jessop's period of office, but only slightly and the per pupil cost of education actually decreased. In 1872-73 the Province's total expenditures on schooling for its 1028 pupils enrolled was $37,763.77, a per pupil cost of $36.73. Five years later for more than twice as many pupils (2198) the total cost was only $43,334.01 or $19.90 per pupil. However, in terms of the total expenditure of the province the portion spent on schools had increased from 5.9% in 1872 to 9.7% in 1878 so the Government was seeking some alternate means of acquiring revenues for school purposes. In his second report Jessop had suggested setting aside "a large portion of the proceeds of land sales . . . not in aid of any particular locality but for the benefit of the Province at large."[30]

Nothing came of this suggestion but in 1876 the Elliott Government passed the controversial School Tax Bill which imposed a poll tax of three dollars per year on every male resident over eighteen years of age to help defray the cost of education. This measure, coming in the same session as the bill which tightened the compulsory education requirement, raised the whole question of whether or not the Roman Catholic minority should have to pay for public education when they preferred to use their own fee-supported parochial schools. The whole issue of the Province's free, non-sectarian school system came under review. Bishop Charles J. Seghers and sixty-three Roman Catholic residents of Victoria presented a petition to the Government stating their objections to the school tax and to the principle of a non-sectarian public school system:

120

That, inasmuch as the so-called unsectarian school system is a flagrant violation of the liberty of conscience, the Catholic portion of this community have but reluctantly submitted to a general system of taxation, a portion of which is set apart for the benefit of the unsectarian schools. But now that it is intended to levy a special tax, your Petitioners view with mistrust and alarm a measure which they deprecate as both unjust and oppressive.

A system of education can never be unsectarian. If it excludes the profession of Christianity, it is anti-Christian; if it does not comprise the belief in God, it is godless and atheistic; if it includes the reading of the Protestant version of the Bible, it is Protestant. Consequently, your Petitioners cannot in conscience send their children to the so-called unsectarian schools, wherever they have schools of their own.[31]

Despite these objections the School Tax Bill passed by a vote of seventeen to six, although this same issue was to be aired on various occasions later.

The annual inspection of his growing school system took up a great deal of Jessop's time as well as imposing a physical ordeal of no small nature. Travelling in the Province in the 1870's he used steamboats and canoes to visit up-Island and lower mainland points and stage coach and horseback in the interior. A few random entries from his diary are eloquent of the difficulties of the travelling inspector:

"May 14 (1874). Down to the Fountain and over Fountain trail to Salsbury's. Left mare and went on foot to Robert — 6 miles — Talked with him about aid for school applied for early in the spring — only about 6 children of school age; Travelled 35 miles."

"May 15 (1874). To Lillooet over the Big Slide — started at 4 a.m. (on horseback), reached Lillooet at 10 — visited school till 1 p.m. — Found 14 pupils in attendance all quiet and orderly — school much improved . . . only beginners — Went to 21 Mile House in the evening — Travelled 35 miles."

"May 16 (1874). Started for Big Bar Creek up the Fraser — failed to get over a creek about eight miles from 21 Mile House on account of bridge being gone — attempted to scale the mountain and cross over to wagon road but could not accomplish it on account of slide — Returned and crossed Pavilion Mountain to Kelly's — Travelled more than 30 miles but only 16 on my journey."[32]

When he returned from his spring tour of the interior in 1876 the *Colonist* described the trip as "a severe one, much more so than any of former years, owing to the limited time at his disposal and the unprecedented high stage of water in the Fraser and its tributaries. Travelling from 40 to 60 miles a day from Okanagan Mission to Yale over rough roads and still rougher trails, with the thermometer ranging from 98 to 106 degrees in the shade was no easy matter. Still greater difficulties had to be overcome in getting past the worst portion of submerged road between the 19 and 20 mile posts. With animals this can only be accomplished by crossing a rugged and precipitous mountain, the summit covered with new snow several feet in depth."[33]

The appointment of Clemitson as his deputy in 1876 gave Jessop much-needed assistance in his duties of inspecting schools and permitted him to devote more of his time to other problems of administration. For an inspector of schools, Clemitson appears to have been somewhat eccentric — although eccentrics in education seem to have been more common in those days than in our enlightened times. One entry in his diary reads "Feb. 21 (1878) I. B. called me a nasty mean fellow. Why?" Another entry records "Sunday March 17, 1878. I, R. M. Clemitson, being of sound mental and bodily health, do hereby pledge myself to abstain from the use of intoxicating liquors and tobacco. In witness whereof I place my signature. R. M. Clemitson, Maple Ridge, B.C." On another occasion his diary contains a draft of a poem he had been composing which began:

> "Dear Frank, the noblest path of life
> Is that prescribed by duty
> And though beset with toil and strife
> That path may glow with beauty.
>
> True hearts can make the darkest day
> Shine with divinest luster
> Around the Christian's upward way
> Faith's brightest glories cluster."

Riding long distances from place to place he had ample time to indulge in another of his little eccentricities that of composing mathematical puzzlers to tax the abilities of some of the better pupils. For example: "What is the double of which as much above 40 as the half below 40 equals 32?" or "A had £80, B £30, and B gave away a certain sum and A twice as much — then A had 3 times as much as B. How much did A give away?"[34]

Jessop was still a busy man. During the year 1866-67 he made sixty official visits throughout the province and conducted single-handed the business of his Education Office where he received 867 letters and wrote another 673.[35] His days were full and his work was satisfying but not without its tensions and strains. In 1877, his seventh year in office, he was granted his first vacation. Under the heading " A Well-Earned Vacation" the *Colonist* observed that, "John Jessop, Esq., Provincial Superintendent of Education, has obtained leave and will sail by the first mail ship for Canada and probably England . . . Under his superintendence the Free School system of the province has in a few years attained a degree of efficiency and importance which enables it to compare favorably with any of them in force in other Provinces . . . We hope that he may enjoy every day of his holiday and that he may return to the Province with his mind filled with valuable information as to the working of the Ontario and English school systems."[36]

Jessop was away from Victoria from October to December inclusive. He apparently did not return to England. His trip was somewhat of a "busman's holiday" as he seems to have used his time in eastern Canada recruiting teachers and visiting prominent persons in the educational field. It is recorded, for example, that he saw Sir John A. Macdonald in Ontario in December[37] and in Fredericton he visited Dr. Theodore Harding Rand, New Brunswick's Superintendent of Education, a man who had the unique distinction of filling this office in two provinces — Nova Scotia and New Brunswick. He was later to move to Ontario where he was a founder of McMaster University. One could almost feel safe in assuming that while in Ontario Jessop would not fail to visit the educator he so much admired, Egerton Ryerson — now retired, and also his long time deputy and successor in office, Dr. J. George Hodgins.

FOOTNOTES

[1] Sixth Annual Report of the Superintendent of Education, 1876-77, p. 12.
[2] Gosnell, R. E., *The Year Book of British Columbia,* Victoria, 1903, p. 257.
[3] Jessop to Hodgins, Victoria, April 27, 1872. B.C. Archives. The Journal referred to was Canada's first education publication—*The Journal of Education of Upper Canada* edited by Ryerson and Hodgins (1848-1877).
[4] Fifth Annual Report of the Superintendent of Education, 1875-76, p. 88.
[5] Sixth Annual Report of the Superintendent of Education, 1876-77, p. 12.

[6] Fourth Annual Report of the Superintendent of Education, 1874-75, pp. 83, 84.

[7] Stubbs, Gordon T., *The Role of Egerton Ryerson in the Development of Public Library Service in Ontario,* Canadian Library Assoc., April 1966, p. 25.

[8] *Ibid.,* p. 23.

[9] Sixth Annual Report, 1876-77, p. 12.

[10] Sumas(s) Lake no longer exists. It was a shallow, marshy lake reclaimed for farm land in 1918 by the Sumas Reclamation Project.

[11] Gosnell, R. E., *The Year of British Columbia,* Victoria, 1903, p. 263.

[12] Third Annual Report of the Superintendent of Education, 1873-74, pp. 19, 20.

[13] *Colonist,* Sept. 7, 1873, p. 3 and Sept. 9, 1873, p. 3.

[14] *Colonist,* January 15, 1875, p. 2. "Nanaimo vs. Victoria".

[15] *Ibid.,* Jan. 19, 1875, p. 3. "Nanaimo vs. Victoria".

[16] Department of Education Correspondence, Microfilm, B.C. Archives.

[17] Third Annual Report of the Superintendent of Education, 1873-74, p. 19.

[18] Fourth Annual Report, 1874-75, p. 90, and *Colonist,* May 11, 1876, p. 3. This building was demolished in 1954. Its bell is mounted in the present Central Junior High School which was erected on the same grounds.

[20] *Ibid.,* Apendix F, p. 157.

[21] Board of Education, Correspondence Outward, 1872-73, and Board Minutes, 1875, April 6. B.C. Archives.

[22] Second Annual Report, pp. 9, 10.

[23] Third Annual Report, p. 25.

[24] Sessional Papers of British Columbia, 1877, p. 142.

[25] An Act Respecting Public Schools, 1872, Section 7 (11).

[26] *Colonist,* May 10, 1872, p. 3.

[27] *Colonist,* May 11, 1876, p. 3.

[28] Fourth Annual Report, 1874-75, pp. 81, 82.

[29] Third Annual Report, 1873-74, p. 21.

[30] Second Annual Report, 1872-73, p. 9.

[31] Sessional Papers of the Province of British Columbia, 1876, p. 725.

[32] Jessop, John, Diary, B.C. Archives.

[33] *Colonist,* June 22, 1876, p. 3.

[34] Diary of R. M. Clemitson, School Inspector 1876-1877, B.C. Archives.

[35] Sixth Annual Report, 1876-77, p. 9.

[36] *Colonist,* Oct. 7, 1877, p. 3.

[37] Jessop to Macdonald, Victoria, Feb. 28, 1879. Public Archives of Canada.

CHAPTER ELEVEN

The First High School

In the first few years of his superintendency Jessop's immediate concern was to provide all children in the province with the opportunity to acquire a common school education. Only when an elementary system had been established could he then turn his attention to the provision of a secondary stage for the select few who on graduation from the common schools might seek further education.

The question of establishing the first high school was discussed by the Board of Education in April 1874.[1] Victoria was considered the only appropriate center but the matter seemed at that time a little premature and after discussion the project was postponed to a later date. However, in September of that year in his annual report Jessop urged that, "The question of High Schools is one that ought not to be left any longer in abeyance. Boys and girls in many parts of the Province are getting ahead of the public school curriculum; not that the teachers in our principal schools are unable to give instruction in the higher branches of an English education, and to make the senior pupils of both sexes much more proficient than they are now."[2] He proposed opening two schools, one in Victoria and the other in New Westminster. These would be provincial institutions built by the Government and administered directly under the Department of Education. They would naturally be small at first. "Each might be commenced with one properly qualified master, and the teaching staff afterwards increased as the attendance might warrant."

He saw these high schools fulfilling a dual role. Not only would they offer further studies to young people, especially those preparing for the professions but they would also "do good service as Training Institutes for teachers, till such time as the number of our school districts would warrant the establishment of a Provincial Normal School . . . These proposed establishments would, therefore, for the present, answers the purposes of High Schools, Training Schools and Model Schools."

He had an interesting proposal to make regarding the site of the New Westminster High School. Since the union of the two colonies the former Government House in New Westminster, where Governor Seymour had resided, had been untenanted. A large and attractive L-shaped building with a verandah at the ground level, dormer windows on the upper floor and a typical Victorian tower, it stood on the river bank east of the town amid pleasant gardens presenting a touch of English elegance in contrast to the simple crudities of the pioneer town. "It would require but little fitting up, in order to make it a very commodious school building and Principal's residence, with excellent accommodation for twenty or twenty-five boarders; the grounds and quiet surroundings are also admirably adapted for such use." With Confederation, title to the property had passed from the Imperial Government to the Dominion Government. Jessop suggested that "a reconveyance of these premises to the Local Government by the Dominion authorities for a High School, would be a most valuable acquisition; and certainly they could not be applied to a better purpose, or one more worthy of encouragement by all concerned."

Whether or not this proposal was passed on to the Dominion Government is not known. At any rate the Board seems to have considered the need for a high school in New Westminster less pressing than for the one in Victoria and it was not until 1884 that the New Westminster High School was opened and then not in the old Government House. In fact by this time the once gracious little Government House, untenanted and untended for eighteen years, had become a dilapidated ruin, its once lovely English garden a tangle of weeds and brush.

In the fall of 1875 the Board of Education began making preparations for establishing a high school in Victoria. It advertised for a master and selected from the nine applicants for the post the Reverend A. B. Nicholson, a B.A. from Queen's University, Ontario.[3] In England, but less so in Canada, it was very common and almost a tradition for grammar school masters to be clergymen. The Board next approved a list of textbooks for the new high school, and by the same token its curriculum.[4]

Should students pay fees for a High School education or would the Board be empowered to extend the free public schooling provided by the Act through the High School grades? This was a nice question which was settled only after test cases and legal battles in Britain and the United States.[5] In his Annual Report for 1873-74 Jessop, always hitherto a supporter of free schooling, was himself in some doubt on this point. "The question as to whether High Schools should be entirely supported by the grant for educational purposes, or whether they should only be aided is an open one, upon which I shall not enter. That poor but talented and deserving pupils should have easy admission to them, few will deny. It is quite a debatable point, however, as to how far the property of all ought to be taxed to pay for the higher education of a few."[6] He had also sought legal advice as to whether the Board had authority to charge fees according to the Public School legislation and in a letter to the Provincial Secretary in January 1876 he suggested the advisability of changing the Act to admit of a small high school fee but giving free tuition to those preparing for teaching. This group, he felt, should also be given some financial aid.[7]

The establishment of a secondary stage to the school system necessitated the institution of Departmental examinations, in this case to determine what pupils were sufficiently well grounded in the elementary subjects to be accepted into the high school. The first of such examinations which were to harass young British Columbians for many years were held in the twenty-one public schools of the province in the spring of 1876. Those not at the time attending the public schools could write the examination in July either in Victoria or in New Westminster.[8]

Candidates were required to write papers in four subjects, i.e., Arithmetic, English Grammar, Spelling and Geography. Some of the questions asked in the arithmetic examinations were: "How long would it take to count a million coins, at the rate of 100 a minute?" "Multiply 5 acres 3 rods 27 poles by 70." "Find the least common multiple of the numbers 8, 12, 18, 24, 27." "Change CMXCIC into Arabic numerals." The English Grammar examination posed such questions as: "What is a Relative Pronoun? What is the usage of *that* as a Relative Pronoun; what other parts of speech might it be?" "Correct where necessary and give rules for — (1) Between you and I. (2) I know that it is her. (3) They thought them to be us" "Parse the italicized words — (1) Tell me *what* you did. (2) *The sun having risen,* we departed." In Geography the pupils were asked among other questions, "How do we know that the earth is round?" "What is longitude; and why do the degrees of longitude differ in length?" "What countries would be passed in sailing from Montreal, Quebec, to Victoria, British Columbia?" The total spelling test (time, half an hour) was to rewrite correctly the following:

"This as a grand and sollem picture, highly sugestif and full of deep feeling and elloquent expresiveness, and most beutifuly illustritiv of the idea saught to be convayed by the poit who rote:
Now faids the glimring lanskip on the site
And all the air a sollem stilnes holds."[9]

Of the 160 candidates who sat for these first "Entrance Examinations" only 68 passed, a failure rate of 58%. Three quarters of the successful candidates were from Victoria and its environs. Only 14 who passed resided outside the capital. There was on this basis hardly any need for a high school in New Westminster. Jessop was somewhat apologetic over the results. It was a low percentage of passes, he conceded, "but future examinations will be certain to make a more favourable exhibit."[10]

The leading student of the province was "Master" John Newbury of Victoria with a 92½% average. Second place went to Miss Mary Anderson with 90%.[11]

The official opening of the province's first high school took place on August 7, 1876. There was little fanfare. The high school had to share the accommodations of the new public school until it could have a building of its own. The *Colonist* described the event briefly:

The pupils of the High School, male and female, numbering in all about seventy, assembled this morning to commence their course of study. The Principal, Mr. Nicholson, in a brief and pithy inauguration pointed out to the young people the many ways he himself had found for acquiring and retaining knowledge. We are slowly of opinion that Mr. Nicholson will be found 'the right man in the right place' and that he will imbue his scholars with a love of learning as well as of all that is good and noble in youthful age.[12]

Only a month after he had taken over the new high school as principal, the Reverend Mr. Nicholson ran into difficulties with the Provincial Board of Education. The point at issue was the place of religion and religious exercises in an ostensibly nonsectarian school system. In the beginning years of the provincial system the Board had chosen to consider "nonsectarianism" as Christianity without bias toward any particular denomination or dogma, and in the light of this interpretation had prescribed certain prayers to be used in

128

addition to the Lord's Prayer and Bible readings. Apparently some citizens had taken exception to this and the Board had inserted in the Rules and Regulations for the Schools a note that "opening and closing exercises are now limited to the Lord's Prayer and Ten Commandments and it is optional with the various Trustee Boards whether the same shall be used or not."[13]

The Reverend Mr. Nicholson's zeal as a clergyman overcame his scruples as a teacher of a nonsectarian school and when parents complained on this account Jessop wrote him directing his attention to the fact that the Consolidated Public School Act, 1876 (section 41) required that all public schools "shall be conducted on strictly secular and nonsectarian principles. The highest morality shall be inculcated but no religious dogmas or creed shall be taught."[14] Nicholson replied in a long letter to the effect that he had been interpreting this section in a much broader spirit apparently than did the Board. "The clause 'strictly secular' to which you direct my attention, is not to my mind, sufficiently clear to decide the exclusion of any reference whatever to religious ideas in the process of education". In support of his point he quoted Professor Huxley and "many of the foremost advocates of secular education in England." He objected to "the narrow secular spirit with which our Provincial system, as I am informed, is to be henceforth identified . . . This system is radically wrong in principle. It ignores the constitution of man's being, in which body, soul and intellect are combined and mutually retractive upon each other . . . How the highest morality can be inculcated where the religious nature and sanctions are practically denied seems to me an utter impossibility . . . Holding the views I do on the subject of education, and unwilling by participation in the present system to appear to have any sympathy with its spirit, in submitting this expression of opinion I also hand in my resignation, to take effect from the present date."[15]

The Board accepted Mr. Nicholson's resignation and appointed Mr. S. D. Pope to the high school principalship.

Mr. Nicholson's conscientious objections to the nonsectarianism of the school system might, at any other time, have blown up a storm of controversy in little Victoria with the correspondence columns of the *Colonist* and *Standard* overflowing with the literary outpourings of all the *pro bono publicos*. As it was, the authorities and citizens were wholly preoccupied with the August and September visit of Canada's Governor-General Lord Dufferin and Lady Dufferin.

The immediate purpose of this first vice-regal visit to British Columbia was to save Confederation. Since the defeat of Sir John A. Macdonald's party in 1873 and the accession to power of the Mackenzie Government there had been precious little progress on the railway which had been promised British Columbia under the terms of union. Mackenzie had simply no faith that the small nation of Canada could forge a link of steel across so many miles of wilderness and impenetrable mountain barriers — and why should she for such a meagre provincial population that amounted to perhaps no more than ten thousand whites? To attempt it, he feared, would mean national bankruptcy and ruin. Could it be constructed as an amphibious highway, alternating water routes served by steam boats with stretches of rail? Could it be financed over a longer period of time?

In the face of Mackenzie's "go slow" policy the impatience of British Columbians rose to the boiling point. Victoria had been waiting for a long time for work to begin on the Island end of the railway, since Esquimalt had been selected as the terminus. Premier Walkem, with his Legislature's sanction, went off to London in 1874 to secure the mediation of the Colonial Secretary, Lord Carnarvon, who proposed an extension of the time limit for completion of the railway to the end of 1890, that work should begin immediately on the Esquimalt and Nanaimo link, and that the interior of the province should see some action on surveys and railroad expenditures. Walkem accepted the "Carnarvon terms" but Mackenzie acceded only on condition that they would not involve increased taxation and later offered the province a lump sum of $750,000 in lieu of building the Esquimalt and Nanaimo Railway.[16] British Columbians were furious. In January the legislature rejected Mackenzie's offer and approved a petition to the Queen voicing the province's grievances and asking for secession if the terms of union were not met by the Canadian Government.[17] Walkem's Government fell soon thereafter and A. C. Elliott became the new premier. The Canadian Government decided that this would be an opportune time to send out the Governor General, a very popular personality in eastern Canada, to assess the British Columbia situation and smooth the ruffled tempers of the West.

The Dufferins arrived at Esquimalt on August 15 on H.M.S. *Amethyst* after crossing the continent by rail to San Francisco. Victorians were in festive array to greet them. Regardless of their resentment against the Mackenzie Government, there was no question of their loyalty to the Crown and their enthusiasm in welcoming the tall and handsome Irish Governor-General and his lovely countess. "I think every one of the five thousand inhabitants of Victoria must have been out in the streets", Lady Dufferin noted in her journal.[18] The triumphal procession made its way past numerous decorated arches which had been erected along the route. The inscriptions varied from expressions of loyalty and warm welcome to references to the province's grievances — "Our Railway Iron Rusts", "Railway the Bond of Union", and "Confederated Without Confederation".[19] "The Chinese put up their own arches", observed Lady Dufferin, "and they were very prettily designed. They hung up lanterns in some, and on one there was quite a houseful of little images. When we entered Victoria there was an address. D. replied from the carriage. At present the feeling here is British, but anti-Canadian, on account of the railroad which can't be made yet; so it is not all plain sailing. We were told that on one arch there was written 'Our Railroad or Separation'. The Governor-General was obliged to refuse to go under it."

After ten days of heady social rounds in Victoria, Dufferin and his party left to extend the vice-regal visit to other parts of the province. They inspected the coal mines of Nanaimo, sailed up the coast to the Queen Charlotte Islands and the Indian village of Metlakatla, toured the sawmills at Burrard Inlet, paid a state visit to New Westminster and struck off to the Interior from Yale by coach over the Cariboo Road to Kamloops Lake and by steamboat to Kamloops. They returned to Victoria on September 14.

On the 18th, Lord and Lady Dufferin were scheduled to visit Victoria's new school — a great occasion for which Jessop, the teachers and the pupils had been preparing for weeks. Crowded into the large assembly hall of the public school were the elementary and high school children of Victoria and a large number of invited guests — members of the legislature, the mayor and council, the Board of Education, the Victoria School Board and their wives. The *Standard* described the event in great detail.[20] "The scholars of the High School and the Boys' and Girls' Public Schools had the honour yesterday of receiving His Excellency the Governor-General and Lady Dufferin. At one o'clock His Excellency and the Countess, accompanied by Col. Lyttleton, entered the Girls' School room, in which the scholars were assembled, the visitors present rising to their feet and the children singing the National Anthem." Superintendent Jessop then read an address of welcome in which he said, in part:

131

Although our school system is comparatively in its infancy, yet Your Excellency will observe that British Columbian Governments have not been unmindful of the educational interests of the rising generation.

This is a day that will long be remembered by the pupils now present. They will feel pride in recounting, as one of the most pleasing reminiscences of their school career, the auspicious event of Your Excellencies' visit — a visit that will exercise a more beneficial influence on their minds in the promotion of loyal and devoted attachment to Her Most Gracious Majesty, and to the person and Government of Your Excellency than any lessons, however carefully taught and impressed.

The Governor-General in reply thanked them for this expression of loyalty and the cordial welcome accorded to Lady Dufferin and to himself:

Knowing as I do how great an effect a judicious system of education has upon the mode of life, conduct and morals of all classes, by forming the mind, enlarging the views and raising the tone of those who come under its influence, it is no less my pleasure than my duty to encourage by every means in my power, the mental, intellectual and physical training of the younger inhabitants of this great Dominion, whose success in life must in great measure depend upon the attention they pay not only to their books, but also to the teaching of those lessons of moral restraint and self respect which are inseparably connected with a sound basis of education.[21]

Dufferin then produced three medals — one of silver and two of bronze bearing on one side the profiles of himself and Lady Dufferin and on the reverse the Dufferin coat of arms. These he offered as prizes to be competed for during the ensuing year. He asked that the names of the winners be enrolled in a book kept for that purpose.

In accordance with Dufferin's wish, his medals were subsequently put up for competition, the silver for the leading high school student in the province and the bronze medals for the boy and girl in highest standing in the public schools of Victoria. The first scholarship examinations were scheduled in the midsummer of 1877. "Competition for the Dufferin medals", wrote Jessop, "was very keen. The examinations themselves, both written and oral, were tolerably searching. More than usual interest was manifested in all the proceedings, as evinced by the large number of visitors present during the three days that the oral examinations lasted."[22] The first winner of the Governor-General's medal for the high school was John C. Newbury and the winners from the public school were Herbert C. Carey and Helen Andrews. The medals, in accordance with Dufferin's instructions, were forwarded with the names of the recipients to him in Ottawa where the names were engraved and returned with complimentary letters from the Governor-General personally. This was the beginning of a tradition which is continued to the present day of honoring the leading students in the province.

At the end of the high school's first year of operation Jessop reported his satisfaction with its initial progress. Attendance he considered (60 enrolled and 49 of an average) was "very gratifying". He considered the management to have been efficient and the instruction imparted "thorough and practical". "The curriculum," he wrote, "is as follows":

ENGLISH: Geography, ancient and modern, Grammar, Rhetoric and Composition, Mythology; SCIENTIFIC: Botany, physiology, Natural Philosophy, Astronomy, and Chemistry; MATHEMATICAL: Arithmetic, Algebra, Mensuration, Euclid, and Book-keeping; CLASSICAL: Latin and Greek; MODERN LANGUAGES: French; together with Map drawing, vocal music, etc.[23]

He added in his annual report an interesting little note on the first extra-curricular activities of the high school students:

A Lyceum Club has been organized among the male pupils, who debate once a week after school hours. Considerable interest is manifested in these exercises. Another source of intellectual improvement, common to both sexes, was engaged in during the greater part of the year, namely, the preparation of manuscript newspapers, filled chiefly with original contributions, interspersed with conundrums, etc., etc. The one edited by the boys is called the "Leisure Hour", that by the girls the "Hyacinth". The articles were written as home exercises and read by pupils selected for the purpose semi-monthly. Many of those pieces have been creditable productions, and the conundrums, etc., chiefly of a local character, often witty and amusing.

The year had seen the beginnings of an extension of the public school system beyond the level of the "common" or elementary school. A high school or secondary stage had been added to the system and already Jessop was considering provisions for adult and higher education.

He looked forward to the day when the province would have a teacher-training college, patterned perhaps after the model of the Toronto Normal School but this was not to be achieved until the first year of the twentieth century. In the meantime the high school had assumed the responsibility for training teachers for the public schools. The Consolidated Public School Act of 1876 permitted the establishment of five scholarships of one hundred dollars each as aid for teachers in training at the high school.[24] Promising high school students with "a natural aptitude for teaching" were encouraged to take the teacher-training course. These pupil-teachers devoted one day out of five to work in a public school, a team of five replacing a permanent classroom teacher. This gave them practical experience in the classroom while at the same time effecting a saving for the government of a teacher's salary. At the end of the year the pupil-teachers could compete for the one hundred dollar scholarship and sit for the teachers' qualification examinations. It was, as Jessop well realized, a make-shift scheme for training teachers which would have to suffice until "the Province could afford a Normal School."[25]

Interest in adult education had its early beginnings in British Columbia with the Mechanics Institutes which had been introduced in the colonial period by British immigrants.[26] The Mechanics Institute movement had developed in Britain in response to the needs engendered by the industrial revolution for an educated and technically trained class of workmen and engineers for Britain's mushrooming industrial machine. The first Mechanics Institutes were established as evening classes for workmen in Glasgow and London in 1823. There were Mechanics Institutes in eastern Canada in the 1830's. The first in British Columbia were sponsored as Mechanics and Literary Institutes by the Anglican Church at Hope (in 1859) and at Barkerville in 1869. The church in these cases provided libraries and reading rooms and organized public lectures. Victoria had a Mechanics Institute in 1864 and in 1871, in response to its appeal for public funds, the government passed an Act Respecting Literary Societies and Mechanics Institutes which regularized the incorporation of these societies. The estimates of 1872 and subsequent years provided grants of from seventy-five dollars to two hundred fifty dollars to each institute. There were Mechanics Institutes at various times (in addition to Hope, Barkerville and Victoria) at Nanaimo, Comox,

Cowichan and Moodyville. When the Victoria Mechanics Institute closed down in 1886 it donated its library to the city to form the nucleus of the Victoria Public Library. These institutes in British Columbia served a social, quite as much as an educational need.

Evening schools of a different type to teach basic literacy to adults who had received little or no formal education were first proposed by Jessop. Indeed he had set the first example by himself teaching such evening classes in connection with his own Central School back in 1867. In his annual report for 1876-77 he proposed setting up evening classes of this nature in the three main cities — Victoria, Nanaimo and New Westminster. The evening schools would be open to both sexes but only to those who, because of employment or other reasons, could not attend during the day. The evening student would be charged a fee ("say a dollar per month") to be supplemented by a government grant. "In San Francisco and many other cities", observed Jessop, "evening schools form an important adjunct to the various systems of education adopted. There can hardly be two opinions as to the utility of such institutions . . .". Such schools would benefit the young men "not only educationally, but it would be the means of keeping many of them from frequenting places where temptations for spending money and acquiring bad habits are almost irresistible."[27]

Not only must the province provide an opportunity for all children to acquire a common school education and for the abler ones to attend a high school, but adults who had been less fortunate in their early lives should have a second chance at a schooling through evening classes. Finally, as high schools were organized in other centres there would soon come from their graduates a demand for a university. In 1877 he was already foreseeing the day when this would crown his educational achievements. "A Provincial University also will speedily become a necessity if British Columbian youth are to be fully prepared for the various avocations of life, without going to other provinces and countries for the purpose of graduating in arts, law and medicine."[28]

FOOTNOTES

[1] Minutes of the Board of Education, April 28, 1874, B.C. Archives.
[2] Third Annual Report, 1873-74, p. 20.
[3] Minutes of the Board of Education, pp. 96 and 104, B.C. Archives.
[4] *Ibid.*, p. 106.
[5] The Cockerton judgement in Britain and the Kalamazoo case in the U.S.A.

[6] Third Annual Report, 1873-74, p. 21.

[7] Jessop, John, Correspondence Outward 1875-77. Letter Book, Aug. 4, 1875 and Jan. 15, 1876. B.C. Archives.

[8] *Colonist,* May 8, 1876, p. 3.

[9] Sessional Papers of the Province of British Columbia, Victoria, 1877, pp. 154-156.

[10] Fifth Annual Report, p. 89.

[11] *Ibid.,* p. 92. John Newbury became a teacher in British Columbia.

[12] *Colonist,* Aug. 8, 1876. Actually the enrolment averaged 44.

[13] Fifth Annual Report, 1875-76, Appendix B, p. 143.

[14] Sessional Papers of the Province of British Columbia, 1877, p. 139.

[15] *Ibid.,* pp. 158, 159. Nicholson to Jessop, Victoria, Sept. 9, 1876.

[16] Ormsby, Margaret A., *British Columbia: A History,* Toronto, MacMillan, 1958, pp. 267-269.

[17] Sessional Papers of British Columbia, 1876, p. 589.

[18] *My Canadian Journal,* Lady Dufferin, Gladys Chandler Walker (ed.), Toronto, Longmans, 1969, p. 200.

[19] *Colonist,* Aug. 18, 1876.

[20] *Standard,* Aug. 19, 1876.

[21] Department of Education papers, Lord Dufferin's address to the schools, B.C. Archives, microfilm.

[22] Sixth Annual Report, 1876-77, p. 14.

[23] *Ibid.,* p. 13.

[24] *Ibid.,* p. 11.

[25] *loc. cit.*

[26] See Johnson, F. H., *A History of Public Education in British Columbia,* U.B.C. Publications Centre, 1964, p. 224ff.

[27] Sixth Annual Report, 1876-77, p. 13.

[28] *Ibid.,* p. 26. Actually the first recorded proposal for a medical school was made by Dr. Helmcken when he was one of the British Columbia delegation to discuss the terms of confederation. In 1870 he proposed that the Dominion Government build a Marine Hospital in Victoria and establish in connection with it a "Medical and Surgical School". (See Ireland, Willard E., "Helmcken's Diary of the Confederation Negotiations, 1870," *B.C. Historical Quarterly,* IV, 3, p. 123.)

CHAPTER TWELVE

Jessop And His Teachers

In the last analysis a school system is only as good as its teachers. If these people are disreputable, ignorant and ill-trained, the children subjected to their teaching and example could hardly be expected to develop into cultured adults or good citizens. No one could appreciate this more than John Jessop who for many years had been a teacher himself. As Superintendent of Education his attitude toward teachers was somewhat ambivalent. He knew from his own experience their problems — their often miserable teaching conditions, their poverty and lack of security and in his sympathy he sought to improve their lot. He also held in his mind an ideal for teachers as a body — the shaping of a profession of teaching — and this would require the elimination of the incompetents from their ranks, the gradual elevation of educational standards for teachers, the introduction of professional training and the development of a professional association and an *esprit de corps.*

One of the first official acts of the newly appointed Board of Education in 1872 had been to confirm the certificates of all teachers then holding posts by granting them all Third Class Certificates. This was a purely temporary measure taken for reasons which Jessop explained in his First Annual Report — "as it was considered necessary firstly that all incumbents of existing schools should qualify in accordance with the existing School Act at once and their schools be brought under the supervision of the Board; and secondly, that longer notice should be given to teachers and others intending to become such, and that papers should be prepared for certificates of a higher grade, embracing a more extended course of studies and more searching examination in each."

By 1873 a certification pattern had been worked out based on examinations prepared by Jessop himself and by the other members of the Board of Education (none of whom had ever taught school). The type of certificate granted depended entirely on the candidate's standing in these examinations, the only exception to this rule being that graduates of British universities were automatically granted First Class certificates. Three classes, each with an A and B level were announced as follows: First Class A for an 80% standing in the certification examinations (or for graduates of British universities), First Class B (70%), Second Class A (60%), Second Class B (50%), Third Class A (40%), Third Class B (30%). The First Class certificates carried permanent tenure. Second Class were valid for three years and Third Class for only one year.

A curious distinction was made between male and female candidates in arriving at these percentages. Two standards were applied. Male candidates' averages were based on their standing in all of the papers whereas for the women the averages were based on all subjects except the mathematical ones, i.e., Euclid, mensuration, algebra and bookkeeping. This seems to have been a typical Victorian concession to members of "the weaker sex" who were considered to be incapable of competing on equal terms with men in those subjects requiring more "mental ability". However, in 1877 the Board abolished this distinction and placed the women and men on an equal basis in computing standings in these examinations.[1]

The first of the annual examinations for teachers was held in the Legislative Assembly Room of the old "Birdcages" in July 1873. Twenty candidates presented themselves, out of whom two failed to gain even a Third Class B certificate. For Interior candidates an examination was held in Clinton with the same set of papers. Only two candidates appeared there for the examinations and only one was successful.

These, the first examinations ever given to teachers in British Columbia, were composed by Jessop and the other members of the Board of Education. They comprised "History and English Literature" (submitted by Dr. S. F. Tolmie), "English Grammar" (A. J. Langley), "Arithmetic" and "Algebra" (R. Williams), "Geography" (M. W. T. Drake), "Bookkeeping, Double Entry" (A. Munro), while Jessop contributed the examinations in "Education and the Art of Teaching", "Vocal Music", "Natural Philosophy", "Euclid", "Animal and Vegetable Physiology" and "Mensuration".[2]

Jessop's examination on "Education and the Art of Teaching" is interesting in that it reveals some of those aspects of teaching which

138

he apparently considered important. It was a two-hour paper consisting of the following eight questions:

1. What is Education? When does it commence and end?
2. Describe what you conceive to be a suitable course for Public School Education in British Columbia.
3. State what you consider the chief characteristics of the successful teacher.
4. What modes of reward do you approve of in the management of schools?
5. What great difference exists between suitable and unsuitable punishments even where both are equally effective in enforcing the required obedience?
6. What beneficial results are attained by written examinations in School? How often and in what manner would you conduct them?
7. Mention the relative duties of Teachers and Parents in the education of children.
8. Should compulsory Education be enforced in the School Districts of this Province? If so, give your reasons.

Similar examinations for the certification of teachers were repeated each summer in the Legislative Assembly Hall and once in New Westminster until the Board of Education was abolished in 1879.

In 1874 he noted that Cedar Hill was "the first and only school in the Province, so far, to send out a teacher from among its pupils — one of them having obtained a certificate of qualification at our last examination who received all her education in this district school."[3]

There have been very few years in Canada's history when the country was not experiencing a shortage of qualified teachers. In the decades of the mid-twentieth century Departments of Education have commonly recruited teachers from other provinces, from the United Kingdom, from Australia, New Zealand and other Commonwealth nations. Jessop faced the same problem in 1874 when he observed that "want of properly trained teachers is a great drawback to the efficiency of the Public Schools of the Province."[4] Of the thirty-six teachers in the employ of his Department at that time only eight had any "regular training for the profession", perhaps as many had some previous experience in teaching but the majority were untrained and inexperienced. The Board of Education had already found it impossible to comply with the regulation in the Public School Act stating that, "No person shall be appointed a teacher in any Public School unless he shall hold a first, second or third class certificate of qualification from the Board of Education." Ruefully Jessop admitted that if this regulation were carried out it would mean the closure of ten or eleven schools.

In the spring of 1873 Jessop had written to his alma mater, the Toronto Normal School, to see if he could recruit a few teachers there, but his offer of salaries of fifty to seventy dollars per month, while high for Ontario, were not considered sufficient to induce the Ontario youth to make the long journey to remote British Columbia.[5]

In 1875 Jessop drew the attention of the Provincial Secretary to the difficulty of obtaining qualified teachers and sought the Government's permission to advertise for teachers in the Ontario press. He added in his letter to the Provincial Secretary that, "It is a question worthy of consideration as to whether or not inducement should be held out to eligible young persons in the shape of aid, if required, in reaching this coast, to be repaid by instalments after obtaining situations."[6] He was granted permission to advertise but the Government would not agree to paying the travelling expenses. Accordingly he drafted the following advertisement which was sent to the Toronto *Globe* and which casts some light on the rural teaching conditions of the time:

RURAL TEACHERS WANTED

A limited number of Second or Third Class teachers, male and female, will find immediate employment in British Columbia at salaries from $50 to $60 per month. The situations are chiefly in newly-formed country districts at present thinly peopled. The schools are small and thus teachers must expect, for a time at least, more or less isolation. Residences are not provided. The cost for board varies from $16 to $25 per month.

Applications to be sent to James Carlyle, Esq., M. D., Normal School, Toronto, who will select from among the applicants as many as are to be provided with situations and give them instructions for proceeding to British Columbia.

John Jessop,
Supt. of Education for B. C.[7]

In an accompanying letter to Dr. Carlyle, Jessop suggested giving the preference to married men with families if such applied. He also advised those intending to come to leave Ontario not later than June 15 in order to be in time for the teachers' certification examinations which were held in early July. This would assume that the travellers would go by rail to San Francisco and by steamer from there to Victoria.

The advertisement occasioned considerable interest resulting in about thirty letters to Dr. Carlyle and numerous enquiries from others who were not teachers but whose interest had been aroused and who were contemplating emigrating to the west coast. Carlyle suggested that the British Columbia Government might do well to consider assisting the immigration of teachers from Ontario as "the expense from Toronto will be about $170, rather a large outlay for many."[8] Mainly because of this factor, many Ontario teachers who would have liked to come to British Columbia balked at the last minute and few teachers actually made the journey from the East. Jessop observed in his next annual report that "seven male and three female teachers have since arrived, chiefly from Ontario and New Brunswick."[9]

Obviously, recruiting out-of-province teachers could at best offer only a temporary and partial solution to the problem of supplying staff for the growing school system. It was this conclusion that was considered by Jessop and his Board when they had decided to establish the first high school and have it serve a dual role as an academy and a teacher-training center. It was essential that British Columbia produce its own teachers and from 1877 on, the high school in Victoria made its modest contribution of graduates to the Province's teaching force. By this date also the supply of teachers had greatly improved. In 1877 British Columbia had seventy-one teachers compared with forty-seven two years before and they were making an effort to upgrade their standing and attain the coveted First Class certificates.[10] Jessop could now write to the Toronto *Globe* and state that his schools were now adequately supplied with teachers and that he expected that "hereafter British Columbia, to a great extent at least, will be in a position to supply her own teachers."[11]

Most of the teachers in Jessop's schools, however, had no training whatsoever. They had been examined and certificated but were not professionally prepared for their work. Jessop planned to give these people some type of in-service training to improve their teaching.

It was obvious to him that, "A Training School will soon become a necessity in this Province; but until such an institution can be established, something might be accomplished in securing uniformity of method by inaugurating Teachers' Conventions or Institutes." At these gatherings he suggested the agenda might include such matters as "time tables and programmes of study . . . and different methods of teaching . . . with a view of adopting some regular system in all schools that may be about equal in attendance and acquirements."[12]

In proposing the establishment of teachers' institutes Jessop was again falling back on his Upper Canadian experience. Teachers' institutes had been convened by Ryerson in Upper Canada since the 1850's for the same purpose as Jessop had in mind, i.e., as a means of furthering the professional education of the teachers and of disseminating the Department's point of view on educational matters.

Accordingly Jessop issued notices of a meeting to make arrangements for annual teachers' conventions. This inaugural meeting was held in July 1874 in the Legislative Assembly Hall with the Hon. Dr. Ash, the Provincial Secretary, in the chair. The aims and purposes of such conventions were discussed and an executive was elected to plan the first of these for July of the following year. Jessop was elected the first President with Vice Presidents Dr. Ash, Rev. Mr. Mason, Principal of the Collegiate School of Victoria, and Robt. Williams, M. A. The Secretary was C. C. Mackenzie, Principal of the Victoria Boys' School and the Treasurer was J. A. Halliday, Principal of the New Westminster Public School. "Among the first beneficial results which I anticipate from the establishment of this convention is the attainment of more uniformity in the methods of teaching. At present the systems prevailing in this Province are as diverse as the nationalities of the teachers. Annual meetings will soon accomplish a great deal in this direction, especially when aided by proper training in the High Schools."[13]

A year later the first British Columbia Teachers' Convention met in the Legislative Assembly Hall. Its three evening sessions were attended by about two dozen teachers (about half of the small teaching force of the Province). They were joined by other citizens interested in education. Papers were read on such topics as "Arithmetic, its Importance as a Branch of Study" (Mr. G. Pottinger of Craigflower), "English Grammar and How I teach It" (Mr. James Kaye, Cedar Hill), "Reading and Our Authorized Text Books" (Mr. John Pleace, Victoria) and "Geography" (Mr. James A. Halliday, New Westminster). Jessop pronounced these papers "all most creditable productions" and was pleased with the "considerable discussion which they stimulated."[14] One of the main topics on the agenda was a discussion of "Graded or Mixed Schools" resulting in the unanimous conclusion that schools should be graded wherever practicable. Jessop was re-elected President for the ensuing year and the other members of the Board of Education were all given vice-presidencies. Teachers filled the offices of Secretary (James Halliday) and Treasurer, with "duties at present *nil*" (John Pleace).

As teachers' conventions in the modern sense of the term these annual meetings in the Legislative chamber bore little resemblance to the professional assemblies of teachers to-day. In the first place they were initiated, sponsored, encouraged, financed and largely directed by the Department of Education. The teachers attended and participated in the agenda but the whole function of these gatherings was to help implement the policies of the Department and bring unity into the educational system. At this time the teachers had no province-wide professional association of their own which could voice their views on educational matters or which could defend or promote their own welfare. However, these Department-centred conventions did bring the province's teachers together and did prepare them to think in terms of their own professional body and in later years to operate their own annual conventions. Already the organization was being called the "British Columbia Teachers' Association"[15] but there was no doubt about it being tied to the apron strings of the Department. Jessop was re-elected each year as president of the association as long as he was Superintendent. However, the accounts of the conventions do show an increasing tendency on the part of teachers to express their own proposals and objectives and not to be overawed by the presence of the Superintendent and members of the Board of Education.

To-day in the 1970's the teaching profession in British Columbia enjoys a respectable salary scale based on the level of education and experience of the teacher. The welfare of its members is protected by a powerful professional association which speaks also with a strong voice on every aspect of education. The teacher has security of tenure and can retire on a well-earned pension.

How different were teaching conditions a century ago! The schoolmaster then had little public recognition as a professional person. With often no more formal education beyond the common school level how could he aspire to a professional status? He belonged to no professional association which could speak for him and protect his salary, tenure or working conditions. He was often paid less than the unskilled laborer. In the year 1876, for example, the Government accounts showed that an assistant gaoler earned $912 per year, a "turnkey" $720, a convict guard $720 and a printer's assistant $758 while the average teacher's salary was $644.41.[16]

Having himself experienced for years the bitter penury of the profession, Jessop was an ardent champion of higher salaries for his teachers. In his annual report of 1873 he pointed out that a teacher earning a salary of fifty dollars a month (the common minimum) could save little. "Board in the outlying districts of Vancouver Island and the Lower Fraser costs about $20 per month; while at Yale and along the Waggon Road it costs double that sum. The teacher's savings, therefore, . . . are very small indeed: much too small to secure and retain the services of really good teachers, particularly males. Common farm hands, if well acquainted with work, can command $50 per month and board, during all the busy portions of the year, thus clearing as much again as the educated school teacher."[17] He recommended that teachers' salaries be increased "at least 20 percent."

In 1874 the Board of Education established a salary scale which paid teachers according to the average attendance of their classes. Those teaching no more than ten to twenty pupils received the minimum salary of $50 per month; from twenty to thirty pupils $60, from thirty to forty pupils $70 and from forty to fifty pupils a maximum salary of $80 per month.[18] This enabled more teachers to earn higher salaries but it obviously discriminated against rural teachers compared with their city colleagues, although the Board tried to compensate for this by a special allowance of $10 per month for "the increased cost of living" for teachers in the Interior beyond Yale. There was, however, another reason behind the new salary scale. Lacking legislation to make schooling compulsory, Jessop was trying to increase the poor school attendance by giving the teacher a powerful stimulus to recruit every school-age child in the neighborhood. Wrote Jessop, "As school-going children and average attendance increase, so will salaries."[19] The following year he reported with some pride that by comparison with other Canadian provinces and certain areas of the United States the average British Columbia teacher was better paid (by $15 a month more than in Oregon, $11 a month more than in California and 100% higher than the average in Ontario, New Brunswick and New York).[20]

Although the Board's regulations stipulated that when the average attendance exceeded fifty pupils, that school would be "entitled" to an extra teacher, nevertheless in some instances school boards did have teachers instructing classes of sixty and even seventy children.[21]

In Jessop's time school vacations were shorter than now. The regulations stipulated that there should be two vacations during the year, one of two weeks at Christmas and New Year and a summer vacation for one month from the first Monday in July or August at the option of the district school board.[22]

In spite of what would seem to be, for those days, good salary inducements, the tenure of teachers in the country districts then, as now, was brief. At Lake School on Vancouver Island, Jessop reported that there had been "no less than sixteen different teachers in little more than five years. Under such circumstances progress can hardly be expected."[23] In other districts one or two changes of teachers annually were not uncommon.

In certain areas of the province, particularly where the inhabitants could not reach agreement on the location of a school, Jessop had to sanction what he considered was a "highly objectionable" arrangement — the "itinerating teachers", instructing children half the time in one place and half in another as happened in North Saanich and South Cowichan.

Living conditions for the rural teachers left much to be desired. Although some districts could offer "teacherages", in most cases the teacher (frequently a young man) would have to board with one of the resident families. The result was perhaps indifferent food and lodging and the loss of the teacher's personal freedom and privacy. "In nearly all our outlying school districts teachers find great difficulty in obtaining board and lodging. Farm houses, in some cases, are too far from the school and in others devoid of accommodation for anyone outside the family." In his second annual report Jessop urged that local boards erect residences for their teachers and that the Government give them fifty percent financial assistance to do so.[24] Two years later he was still trying to interest the school boards in this proposal. Finally his efforts seem to have borne fruit when in 1876 he noted that at Cedar Hill, on land donated by Dr. Tolmie, "a very commodious residence has been added to the School premises which soon will be occupied by the teacher's family.[25] In the same year teachers' residences were being erected also at South Saanich, Gabriola Island and Hope.[26]

In the small British Columbia communities of the 1870's every teacher's personal problems were public knowledge and these often became the concern of the school authorities. The loneliness, the pressures and the frustrations of their lives drove many to the consolation of the bottle — as, for example, the case of the Cowichan teacher who had come to Victoria to write his teachers' qualification examination. He had begun it in the morning, returned intoxicated in the afternoon, remained only a few minutes and left. After seeking further alcoholic surcease, he had the misfortune in the evening to fall off the Hudson's Bay Company's wharf. He was rescued from the harbor and dismissed by the Board of Education. Later Jessop relented and reinstated him in his Cowichan school, but some weeks later another alcoholic interlude resulted in his final dismissal.[27]

Then in 1877 there was the case of S. D. Pope, principal of the high school, who was charged by the Board of Education with reports "prejudicial to his character and sobriety". Warned at the time, he reappeared before the Board the next year, again on charges of "intemperance". When he demanded that written evidence be produced and such was not forthcoming, he resigned.[28]

Another high school master, G. V. De Vaux, who for a time was somewhat of a local hero in Victoria for his action in risking his life to stop a horse which was running away with a woman and her children, fell from favor and was suspended by the Board of Education over a divorce case. He was probably the first British Columbian to publish anything in the field of education. In addition to articles which he contributed to one of Canada's earliest national journals, the *New Dominion Monthly,* he had written a book on *The Science and Art of Teaching.*[29]

Jessop, as we have seen, consistently championed the welfare of his teachers in trying to gain for them higher salaries, some in-service professional training, and better teaching and living conditions. Further evidence of his concern is to be found in his efforts to establish pensions for them. In his Fifth Annual Report (1876) he sketched the first proposal in British Columbia for a teachers' superannuation fund:

> The time has fully arrived for this Province to follow the example of Ontario, Quebec, some of the Australian Colonies, Great Britain and many of the German states, in establishing a Superannuated Teachers' Fund for the benefit of teachers when they have arrived at a certain age in the service. It would be almost superfluous for me to enumerate the many advantages that must accrue to the profession from an arrangement of this description. The following are some of them:— It would form a bond of union among the members. They would have some-

thing to look forward to after a definite period of service. It would act as a powerful inducement not only in encouraging persons of ability and culture to enter the profession, but in retaining them in it for a longer period. Public school teaching would not be regarded as merely a stepping stone to something more remunerative when those engaged in it would be certain of receiving an annual stipend at a fixed age, when they would have the right to retire, or of aid should they be obliged through failing health to relinquish the profession sooner.[30]

He proposed a scheme where the Legislature would appropriate "for the present, say $500 per annum" and to which all qualified teachers would add perhaps 1% of their salaries. It would be a few years before the fund would build up to a respectable pension but he did not anticipate many retirals until then.

His proposal was put before the Teachers' Convention held the following July in the Legislative Assembly Hall and was approved by those present, although some objected to the clause requiring compulsory contributions from all in the profession.[31] A committee was appointed to prepare the details of a superannuation scheme to lay before the teachers' association at the next annual convention. When it met in New Westminster in July 1877 the committee's proposals were approved and a new committee was appointed to place the scheme before the Government.[32] Their pleas, however, fell on deaf ears. The *Colonist* roundly denounced the idea that the Government should contribute public money to the fund. If the teachers wanted a pension fund they should finance it on their own.[33] Jessop's proposal was far ahead of his time. It was not until 1921 that the Government made any effort to provide pensions for teachers.[34]

In his own mind Jessop had developed certain ideals about the profession of the teacher and in his term of office as Superintendent he sought to achieve these. He wished to see his profession raised from its menial status to one commanding the respect of the public. Only by a genuine improvement in their own education and qualifications and by conscientious devotion to their duties could they expect to gain public esteem. Better living and teaching conditions, security and superannuation were essential to attract good people into the profession. But teachers must earn their status. Jessop was a firm believer in a merit system. Merit should be rewarded by higher certification and salaries, by security in employment and by preferment to more desirable posts. He watched carefully the examination results for entrance to high school and considered the success of pupils in these a good indication of their teachers' worth. For those whose pupils did not achieve good results he warned that, "Failures in the future to pass pupils in this competitive examination will be attributed, with but few exceptions, to inefficiency in imparting instruction, or want of attention to school duties and industry in the performance of them. All other things being equal, there can be no excuse for a teacher not having pupils far enough advanced to make a creditable showing at these examinations when the one in the neighbouring district has his or her pupils well up to the requisite standard." [35]

For others who gave faithful service to their pupils and their communities he awarded official praise in his annual reports. Of Miss Adelaide Bailey of Hope he wrote, "Her departure was much regretted by all interested in the school, which here means the entire population." [36] Of Mr. Donald McMillan of Chilliwack: "The teacher is most enthusiastic and painstaking in the work of imparting instruction." [37] Of Mr. A. McKenzie of Okanagan: "The children in this newly-established school are making remarkable progress in their studies, especially when the fact is taken into consideration that many of them when they commenced were almost entirely ignorant of the English language . . . They were quiet and orderly and much attached to their school and their teacher." [38] Of Mr. E. N. Brown of Clinton: "The people of Clinton have reason to be satisfied with the successful working of their school, but they have also reason to congratulate themselves upon having a teacher who, by example as well as precept, exerts a salutary, moral influence which cannot fail to produce a strong and lasting impression upon his pupils." [39]

In these words of praise for "good and faithful servants" Jessop was expressing his own ideals for the teaching profession.

FOOTNOTES

[1] Sixth Annual Report, 1876-77, p. 101.
[2] Second Annual Report, Appendix D.
[3] Third Annual Report, 1873-74, p. 26.
[4] *Ibid.,* p. 24.
[5] *Ibid.,* p. 24.
[6] *Ibid.,* April, 1875.
[7] Jessop to Provincial Secretary, March 22, 1875, Board of Education Correspondence Outward, Letter Book 1873-75, p. 517, B.C. Archives.
[8] Fourth Annual Report, 1874-75, p. 86.
[9] *Ibid.,* p. 84.
[10] Sixth Annual Report, p. 8.

[11] Sessional Papers of British Columbia, 1878, p. 67.

[12] Second Annual Report, p. 8.

[13] Third Annual Report, 1873-74, p. 23.

[14] Fourth Annual Report, 1874-75, p. 89.

[15] See account of the 1877 convention in the Sixth Annual Report, 1876-77, pp. 10 and 11.

[16] Sessional Papers of British Columbia, 1877, pp. 88, 541ff.

[17] Second Annual Report, 1873, pp. 6, 7.

[18] Board of Education Minutes, March 31, 1874, B.C. Archives.

[19] Third Annual Report, 1873-74, p. 25.

[20] Fourth Annual Report, 1874-75, pp. 79, 80.

[21] Third Annual Report, p. 29 and Fourth Annual Report, p. 81.

[22] Fifth Annual Report, 1875-76, p. 141.

[23] Sixth Annual Report, 1876-77, p. 15.

[24] Second Annual Report, 1873, p. 8.

[25] Fifth Annual Report, 1876, p. 100.

[26] *Ibid.*, pp. 101, 104, 109.

[27] Jessop, J., Correspondence Outward, 1874, pp. 264, 269, B.C. Archives.

[28] Board of Education Minutes, July 10, 1877 and June 4, 1878, B.C. Archives.

[29] *Ibid.*, July 10, 1877 and *Colonist,* August 18, 1876.

[30] Fifth Annual Report, 1876, pp. 89, 90.

[31] Sixth Annual Report, 1877, pp. 10, 11.

[32] Superintendent's Annual Report, 1877-78, p. 181.

[33] *Colonist,* March 27, 1877.

[34] See Johnson, F. H., *A History of Public Education in British Columbia,* U.B.C. Publications Centre, 1964, p. 244ff.

[35] Sixth Annual Report, 1876-77, p. 9.

[36] Fifth Annual Report, 1875-76, p. 109.

[37] *Ibid.,* p. 108.

[38] *Ibid.,* p. 109.

[39] Sixth Annual Report, 1877, p. 25.

CHAPTER THIRTEEN

A Victim of Politics

The year 1878 was Jessop's last in office as the Superintendent of Education. He was by now very popular with his teachers, most of whom realized that he had their welfare at heart and respected him as an educator. Inevitably, however, he had made his quota of enemies, some of whom were in high office and quite unscrupulous.

His reputation as an administrator had been tarnished somewhat during the previous two years by the fiasco of the Cache Creek Boarding School, although it is difficult to blame him for any part of that scandal other than perhaps for his unfortunate choice of men as principals of the institution. He was no doubt too trusting. Yet it is difficult to see how he could have foreseen the troubles in which the school was to find itself embroiled.

Criticisms of Jessop were first made in the Legislature when amendments to the School Act were being proposed in 1876. "The efforts of the Opposition, led by three of the late Ministers," stated a *Colonist* editorial, "seemed to be directed towards dismissing the Superintendent, substituting a political head, and a deputy superintendent on the Mainland."[1] The leader of the Opposition at this time was George Anthony Walkem and another of the ex-ministers attacking Jessop was Robert Beaven, formerly Chief Commissioner of Lands and Works under Walkem. Beaven, according to the *Colonist*, "grossly slandered the Superintendent of Education by stating that that officer, in travelling expenses and salary, cost the Province $5000 each year." John Mara came to Jessop's defense in the House and pointed out the inaccuracy of Beaven's statement, giving Jessop's expenses for each year and showing that they averaged only $514 per annum, which, together with Jessop's $2000 salary, was about half the amount that Beaven had cited. "Mr. Mara, then, in most cutting language, proceeded to castigate the ex-chief (Commissioner of Lands and Works) for his misrepresentations, holding him up to the contempt and scorn of the House, as having stated what he must have known to be false, and leaving him so utterly demoralized and 'used up' that he sat through the rest of the day without saying another word."[2]

The Superintendent's supporters had won this skirmish but it was obvious that the Walkem clique had marked Jessop for liquidation should they ever return to power. The Elliott Government, as we have seen, did amend the Act to create the post of Deputy Superintendent to assist Jessop with the supervision of schools in the Interior. Significant changes were also made regarding appointment to the office of Superintendent of Education. The original legislation of 1872 had stated that the Superintendent should receive an annual salary of $2000 together with travelling expenses. The Act of 1876 eliminated reference to any specific amount simply stating that the Superintendent and Deputy Superintendent shall receive "such annual salaries as the Lieutenant-Governor in Council shall deem fit and proper." The original act, apropos the appointment to the office of Superintendent, had included the proviso that "no person shall be eligible for superintendent unless he has been an experienced and successful teacher of at least five years' standing, and holds a first class certificate from some College, School, or Board of Examination in some other Province or Country where a Public School System has been in operation." The new act now left the appointment completely to the direction of the Lieutenant-Governor in Council empowering them to appoint anyone they might consider "a fit and proper person."[3] These amendments obviously weakened Jessop's position. Under a friendly government he had perhaps little to fear but should his enemies come to power he would be completely at their mercy.

The Provincial Board of Education had also come under some criticism in recent years. One anonymous writer to the *Colonist* signing himself "Scholasticus" described the Board as "an effete piece of machinery". "Eliminate the two working members and you could scarcely find five other men in a scholastic point of view who could be more obstructive or more obnoxious than they are. They never visit the schools over which they preside; they are of too high a social rank to condescend to have their children taught with Tom, Dick and Harry; they give away the best scholastic positions in the Province to their friends or to those who have taught their children in private schools, and above all, having arrived here with the prejudices against popular education of the England of twenty years ago, they have retained their opinions and are at present only tolerant to the system of public education established here because of the political pressure brought to bear upon them by us — the *ignobilis vulgus.*" This critic further objected to the "Forms of Prayer" which he considered inappropriate in "our secular non-sectarian schools", to a salary scale which paid "the same salary to the principal of a school of 37 as to one who had a school of 150" and to the requirement in the Act that the Superintendent be a "lecturer or an itinerant preacher after the manner of Ontario".[4]

Jessop, as Secretary of the Board, hastened to his colleagues' defense in the next day's *Colonist* pointing out that the Board meetings had averaged nearly two per month. Only three times in four years had there been no quorum for a meeting. "I pass over all the acerbity and unjust criticism shown by 'Scholasticus'," wrote Jessop, "but I am in duty bound to state that all gentlemen on the Board are willing and anxious at all times to promote the educational interests of the Province at large." [5]

One criticism of the Board was that its members were all Victorians. One of the proposed changes contemplated in 1876 would have included Mainland members on the Board. Jessop was not in favor of this because of the difficulty of these members travelling to Victoria for the frequent meetings. The proposal was then quietly dropped.

Throughout the year 1877 Premier Andrew Charles Elliott navigated a very leaky ship of state only to founder in the election of June 1878. The new premier was George Anthony Walkem.

Walkem had been born in Ireland in 1834 and had come to Canada, to Quebec City, as a child of ten. When the family later settled in Montreal George Anthony was able to attend school, and for a time, McGill University.[6] He then articled with a Montreal law firm and was called to the Lower Canada bar in 1858. In 1861 he moved to Upper Canada and the next year to British Columbia. He had considerable difficulty being admitted to the British Columbia bar due largely to the opposition of the authorities (in particular Chief Justice Begbie) to any but British-trained barristers. This situation was remedied in 1863 and Walkem was finally admitted to practise among the miners of the Cariboo. Here he was popular, and entering politics, won the Cariboo seat in the Colonial Assembly in 1864. He it was who first proposed the official use of the decimal currency in 1865. He supported Confederation with Canada in 1870 and was for a time Attorney General in the first provincial cabinet. When de Cosmos resigned as premier in 1874 Walkem succeeded him and went as premier to England that year to negotiate with Lord Carnarvon for more favorable terms of union with Canada. For a time in 1876, frustrated with the Mackenzie Government's inaction on railroad construction, he actually proposed secession from Canada. His government was defeated later that year and Walkem spent the next two years in opposition. Now, in 1878, he was back in power.

Walkem was a small man physically. In appearace, with spectacles added, he could have passed for Rudyard Kipling. He had a reputation among the Cariboo miners for a certain genial conviviality but few who knew him trusted him. "Inclined to sharp practice" was Sir John A. Macdonald's comment on him.[7] When in 1882 he was appointed to the Supreme Court, the *Colonist*, never an admirer of his, described him as leaving behind "an unsavoury political reputation".[8]

Walkem's new Minister of Finance and Agriculture was Jessop's old *bête noire,* Robert Beaven. From these men Jessop must have realized he could expect no quarter.

Rumors to this effect must have been going the rounds at the annual provincial teachers' convention held in July, (this time in New Westminster). Jessop was present and gave a two-hour talk on his recent journey to eastern Canada.[9] In the concluding session he was reelected President of the Association for the ensuing year and prior to adjournment the teachers presented him with a testimonial "expressing their implicit confidence" in him.

The next day's issue of the Victoria *Standard* contained an anonymous letter signed "Sufferer", ostensibly by one of the teachers. It was critical of Jessop.[10] This letter evoked a reply in the *Colonist,* also anonymous, from one signing himself "Experienced Teacher" in which the writer suggested that "Sufferer" might be either the editor of the *Standard* "or some other ignoramus outside the pale of civilized school teachers, or else we have a traitor among us . . . Every teacher who was at the convention will remember having signed a testimonial to the Superintendent of Education. Now if there be a teacher who has so far forgotten all that pertains to honesty, uprightness and integrity as to one day sign a testimonial praiseworthy of the Superintendent and his administration and the very next write, as 'Sufferer' has done, in disparagement of the same and who also is as illiterate as 'Sufferer' seems to be, judging from his composition, he ought to be dismissed from the staff *sans ceremonie* and at once. I am ashamed of him as a brother teacher."[11]

Jessop was not left long in doubt as to the new Government's intentions for his Department. In July proposals for amending the School Act were placed before the Board of Education with which that body could not concur. There is no record, either in existing correspondence or in the Board Minutes as to the nature of these preliminary proposals but they obviously would put an end to the function of the Board as a relatively independent body. The Board could not accept the changes and all members, except for the Superintendent, resigned.

On August 23 a resolution of the Committee of Supply was placed before the House to reduce the Superintendent's salary to $750 for the half year ending December 31, 1878. William Smithe, then leader of the opposition and later to become the sixth premier of British Columbia, rose to the defense of the Superintendent. As reported in the *Colonist*:

> Mr. Smithe asked that the Government would reconsider this vote and increase his salary. It was an important office and one entailing a large amount of responsibility. He has to work at almost all hours of the day and often at night. He has done his work on the whole well and established the educational system of the Province satisfactorily. It was not right that he should be placed exactly on the same footing as those under him. The high school teacher is put down for the same salary and has nothing like the same responsibility, besides having easier working hours from 9 a.m. to 3 p.m., one day in every week a holiday and the usual term vacations. The Superintendent's hours are from Monday morning till Saturday night and from January 1st to December 31. He thought fairness required some slight advance to be made. (Hear).
>
> Hon. Mr. Walkem said that if the hon. gentleman had been a friend of the superintendent he would have allowed this vote to pass without comment. He then proceeded to refer to that gentleman's appointment and characterised the Act under which that took place as a disgrace to the community. Some two years since he had called the attention of the late Government to this matter and had asked them to appoint some gentleman who was well acquainted with the working of the school system, and the present Government would see that this took place. He made some very uncomplimentary personal allusions to Mr. Jessop.[13]

The *Colonist* did not detail these specific "personal allusions" made by the Premier but from the other Victoria paper, the *Standard*, we learn that Walkem charged Jessop with being "unfit in point of education for the position he held". He had read the Superintendent's Report of 1876 and criticized it for its errors of expression. "There were in a few pages of the report over 300 blunders. Not to be hypercritical, there were at least that number of grammatical errors and liberties taken with the language . . . He (Mr. W.) then gave an amusing history of the canvass and lobbying amongst members in 1872 which led or rather forced Mr. McCreight's Government to appoint Mr. Jessop against their inclinations and of the School Act which was passed by the House and at the instance of one of the Ministers in order to confer the position upon the present incumbent, whose certificate was an old one and of a class that would not at the present day be granted for the same limited knowledge as it then guaranteed." [14]

There might well have been some basis for the charge of lobbying in 1872. It was a commonplace of political life then as it is to-day. But Walkem's claim that in a few pages of one of Jessop's reports he had counted over 300 "blunders" and at least as many grammatical errors was so fantastic and impossible as to defy the credence of even the most gullible listener.

Various other members of the House rose in Jessop's defense. Helgeson paid tribute to Jessop's education and conscientious devotion to the school system and claimed that the cry against him came from persons in Victoria who were envious of his position. McGillivray endorsed these opinions and spoke favorably of the quality of the lectures which he had heard Jessop deliver. Harris said the Superintendent had given "universal satisfaction in his district". John Mara, who had defended Jessop two years previously, claimed that "on the Mainland and in the rural districts of the Island he was not only popular, but looked upon as having brought the school system to its existing state of efficiency".

Smithe spoke again saying that the present incumbent had performed his duties well and to the satisfaction of the larger number of persons and he thought it would be unjust to remove him. He distinctly recollected the passing of the act under which the present incumbent was appointed and the fact that Mr. Jessop's claims to that position were considered by a Government of which the Hon. Mr. Walkem was a member showed his qualifications at that time were considered good and the past seven years had proved that the appointment had been a good one. [15]

A hard-hitting editorial in the *Colonist* of August 25 termed the

"ferocious assault by the Premier on the Superintendent of Education
. . . one of the most disgraceful incidents of the session, the coarse
and undignified language used by Mr. Walkem towards an old and
faithful public servant who has devoted the best years of his life to
founding a system of education that will remain as an enduring
monument to his genius and assiduity, meets with universal condem-
nation".[16]

But Jessop's defenders were voices crying in a political wilderness.
The vote was passed by the House. After a gloomy weekend of sad
contemplation a discouraged Superintendent went to his office on
Monday and composed his resignation:[17]

Education Office 26th Augst 1878.

Sir

I have the honor to place in your hands my resignation of
the office of Superintendent of Education for the Province of
British Columbia, which it has been my privilege to hold for
nearly seven years.

I am constrained to take this step in consequence of the
observations made by the Hon. the Premier in the Legislative
Assembly on Friday last.

I regret that the Hon. the leader of the Government thought
fit to take the unusual course of attacking my official reputation
in the House of Assembly without having in any way, or at any
period, intimated to me that my work was not satisfactory.
At the same time I feel assured that on inspection of what I
have done educationally, as shown by School Reports in the
Sessional Papers, every candid and honorable mind will come to
the conclusion that the Premier's remarks were unwarrantable.

I have the honor to be
Sir
Your very obt. servt.
John Jessop

Hon. Provincial Secretary

The following day the *Colonist* reported the Superintendent's
resignation to the public and in an editorial valediction expressed
the respect which most citizens of the Province felt for John Jessop:[18]

Mr. Jessop was the first Superintendent of Education after
Confederation. He took up the work when school matters were
in an inchoate and confused state, and by sheer force of an iron

will and untiring energy has raised free education to its present efficiency. Where before there were but half-a-dozen schools scattered over a wide expanse of territory, with the teachers as fitful as the attendance; where neither order, system nor regularity was observed; where the buildings were mean and dilapidated; where teachers and scholars came and went when and where they liked with a sovereign contempt for the timepiece; and where the education imparted was generally of a crude, backwoods character, we find order and system introduced, with as fine schools and as excellent advantages for imparting instruction as are possessed by any Province of the Dominion.

The editorial quoted liberally from the statistics of Jessop's last report to show the present size of the school sytem and the magnitude of Jessop's duties.

Grass could not grow under the feet nor moss accumulate on the finger-ends of a man whose time was so busily employed as Mr. Jessop's. His duties, with a salary one-half as large, were more onerous and responsible — more difficult and unremitting — than those of any Cabinet Minister. When in town he was found at his office attending to his duties at all hours. If called to the inaccessible interior he braved every difficulty and danger and underwent every privation in the strict discharge of his duty. His heart was in his work. He felt interested in making it a grand success. He started out determined to disarm prejudice, to defeat the machinations of many who prophesied that free education would not flourish in Columbia and to place within the reach of every man's child in the Province the priceless boon of free education. He has accomplished his purpose. More than that, he has been scrupulously honest in the disbursement of the monies entrusted to him . . . . His worst enemies — always on the alert to pick flaws in his administration — have breathed no word against his integrity . . . All that Mr. Walkem could find to say against him was that his report of 1876 was ungrammatical . . . Mr. Jessop retires from office covered with honor, and the plaudits of a grateful people will follow him into the shades of retirement.

The *Nanaimo Free Press* added its note of appreciation for Jessop's services. "Mr. Jessop has been a faithful, energetic and efficient officer . . . While perhaps a successor to Mr. Jessop may be found higher in the classics, etc., it will be hard to find one who will so devotedly attend to the onerous duties of Superintendent of Education."[19]

FOOTNOTES

[1] *Colonist,* Aug. 11, 1876, p. 2.

[2] *Ibid.*

[3] An Act to Amend and Consolidate the "Public Schools Acts", 1876, section 5,

[4] Scholasticus, "Free Schools — What is Wanted", *Colonist,* May 8, 1876, p. 3.

[5] Jessop, John, "The Board of Education", *Colonist,* May 9, 1876, p. 3.

[6] Jackman, S. W., *Portraits of the Premiers,* Sidney, Gray's Publishing Co., 1969, pp. 31-40.

[7] *Ibid.,* p. 40.

[8] *Ibid.,* p. 31.

[9] *Colonist,* July 18, 1878, p. 3.

[10] *Standard,* July 18, 1878, p. 3.

[11] *Colonist,* July 19, 1878, p. 3.

[12] Kerr, J. B., "John Jessop", *Biographical Dictionary of Well-Known British Columbians,* Vancouver, Kerr and Begg, 1895, p. 208.

[13] *Colonist,* Aug. 24, 1878.

[14] *Standard,* Aug. 24, 1878. (To find the "300 blunders" referred to by Walkem in Jessop's 1876 report would assuredly defeat the efforts of even the most pedantic of academic purists.)

[15] *Colonist,* Aug. 24, 1878.

[16] *Colonist,* Aug. 24, 1878.

[17] B.C. Archives, Provincial Secretary — Board of Education, Correspondence Outward Letter Book, 1877-79.

[18] *Colonist,* Aug. 27, 1878, p. 2.

[19] *Nanaimo Free Press,* Aug. 28, 1878.

CHAPTER FOURTEEN

Later Years

Following the resignation of Jessop and the entire Board of Education, the Government proceeded to effect certain changes in the administrative structure of the Department of Education. Perhaps by design or perhaps by coincidence these followed the pattern of similar changes which had been made in Ontario on the retirement of Dr. Ryerson in 1876. The powers and duties of the former Board of Education were now transferred to the Lieutenant-Governor-in-Council (i.e., the Government). The position of Superintendent of Education was retained but as the executive officer of the Government in education. The Department of Education had as yet no Minister of its own. The Provincial Secretary continued in this role until 1891 when the Hon. James Baker became the first Minister of Education. The Superintendent was to be given the assistance of one or more school inspectors but no such appointments were made until 1887 when a New Westminster principal, Mr. D. Wilson, became the first full-time provincial inspector.[1] The new Public School Act of 1879 further increased the authority of the local school boards giving them the unchallenged right to hire and fire their own teachers.

Jessop's immediate successor to the office of Superintendent was C. C. Mackenzie, principal of the Victoria Boys' School. He was a Scottish M.A. who had been teaching in the province since 1872.

Dejected but not discouraged, Jessop had now to find himself other employment. He had, in the past, tried teaching, mining, printing and administration. What should it now be? His pride prevented him from returning to teaching. Officialdom of some kind appealed to him but there would be no hope of further employment with the Government of British Columbia, at least as long as Walkem was in power. He turned to Ottawa for help, and after a winter of unemployment, appealed to Sir John A. Macdonald. The Canadian premier had just recently won the national election of 1878 but had been personally defeated in his home constituency of Kingston. He had, however, been offered the seat in Victoria and now represented that British Columbia riding in parliament. Jessop was writing to the Prime Minister, therefore, as his own M.P.:

Victoria, B.C., Feb. 28, 1879.

Sir,

Early in Dec. last I forwarded an application to the Hon. the Post Master General for the appointment of chief clerk in the P.O. here rendered vacant by the death of the former incumbent. As no reply has yet been received I beg to address you a few lines with reference thereto—

Since I had the honor of a short conversation with you in Toronto in Dec. 1877, a change of government here obliged me to resign the position I then held as Supt. of Education for this Province — an unsuccessful contest for a seat in Parliament in the Conservative interest left me without employment, and I shall therefore be glad to obtain the situation already applied for, or failing that, any other in this Province in the gift of your government for which I may be qualified.

I am very reluctant to enlist in the army of office-seekers; but having spent several years in official life and nearly 20 in this city, I am unwilling "to go into trade" — May I venture to hope, therefore, that, as one of your own constituents and earnest supporters since 1850 may I be honored with your favourable consideration?

Should references be required I may mention the names of Senators Carrall, Macdonald and Cornwall — Messrs. Dewdney, J. S. Thompson and McInnes, M.P.'s for this Province, and Messrs. A. M. Sandon and I. Hubert Mason, Toronto . . .

Right Honourable Sir
John A. Macdonald
Ottawa

I have the honor to be
Sir
Your very obv. servt.
John Jessop[2]

There is no record of a reply from Sir John A. Macdonald and the position he sought went to someone else.

Jessop had tried for some considerable time to collect salary arrears from the Government. In November 1879, over a year after his resignation, his claims against the Government for money owed him were still unsettled.[3]

Failing to find any other suitable employment, Jessop returned once more to the publishing trade. He was employed in the office of the Victoria *Colonist* for approximately two years.[4]

The Walkem government was sputtering to an end in 1882 when George Anthony Walkem escaped the final debacle through his appointment to the Supreme Court. His friend and cabinet colleague, Robert Beaven, succeeded briefly to power but the Beaven-Walkem faction was repudiated by the people in 1883 and Beaven resigned the leadership to William Smithe. John Robson became the new Provincial Secretary and Minister of Agriculture.

Robson had been an old friend of Jessop's for over twenty years and it will be recalled how Smithe, as opposition leader, had defended Jessop in the House against the calumnies of Walkem. Thus the local political climate was once more favorable to Jessop, and when the Government decided to establish a Bureau of Immigration and Agriculture under Robson's Ministry this may well explain the gazetting on March 29, 1883 of John Jessop as the first Provincial Immigration Agent. The *Colonist* praised the appointment:

Immigration Agent

The govt. made a wise selection in the appointment of Mr. Jessop as immigration agent. There has never been in the history of the province an occasion when an enlightened and systematic policy for receiving immigrants and conducting or directing them to favourable locations was more needed. Heretofore immigrants have been left to shift for themselves. Neither map nor handbook was provided for their information and if any applied to the government for land they were nearly always chilled by the cool treatment they received. In the appointment of Mr. Jessop the government have shown that they appreciate the importance of the present opportunity for settling the country. Mr. Jessop is thoroughly acquainted with all parts of the province, its resources and capabilities. He is eminently practical and will devote his time and energy to further the good object the government have in view. No better selection could have been made.[5]

An agency of this nature had been suggested in the widely-read book, *Ocean to Ocean,* by the Reverend George M. Grant, principal of Queens University. It was the account of the Sandford Fleming expedition to explore a railroad route from the east to the west coast. In it Grant had drawn attention to the need for an immigration agency on the west coast:[6]

> There is little or no immigration to Vancouver's Island, and little has been done to induce it, or to smooth the way for those who arrive. When an immigrant reaches the country he finds it difficult to obtain information as to where there is good land to take up; and how is it possible for him to go out among a sea of mountains to search for a farm? The island should be thoroughly surveyed according to the simple system long practised in the United States, and lately adopted in Manitoba; the amount of good land known, divided into sections and subsections, and numbered; so that on arriving at Victoria, the immigrant could go into the Crown Land office, learn what land was preempted, and where it could be expedient for him to settle. There are many obstacles in the way of immigrants reaching this distant colony, and therefore special efforts are required to bring them, and to keep them when they come; for until there is a large agricultural population, the wealth of the country must continue to be drained out of it, to buy the necessaries of life and every other article of consumption, from Oregon, California, Great Britain, and elsewhere.

It would be interesting to know whether or not the decision to open an immigration office in Victoria was in response to Grant's suggestion or arrived at quite independently. In his first year as Immigration Agent Jessop did correspond with Principal Grant.[7]

Jessop's first report to John Robson (1883) will illustrate the nature of his duties. He collected statistics on immigration into the province, handled correspondence with intending immigrants and distributed thousands of handbooks on the provinces' resources, its potentialities for settlement, its agriculture, industries and employment needs. He noted in 1883 that white immigration for that year was approximately 6000 and Chinese immigration another 3000. He drew attention to the housing shortage throughout the province as constituting a serious problem for the growing influx of settlers expected to flock into British Columbia with the completion of the Canadian Pacific Railway. The east coast of Vancouver Island, he noted, now seemed to offer good agricultural lands and, with the construction of the Esquimalt and Nanaimo Railway, tempting inducements for settlers.[8]

In 1884 the Immigration Agency was transferred from provincial to federal authority and placed under the Dominion Ministry of Agriculture. Jessop now became the Dominion Immigration Agent. His report of 1884 addressed to the Minister of Agriculture at Ottawa was actually published in the Sessional Papers of British Columbia as "being of much interest and containing valuable statistical information respecting the Province.[9]

For the next fifteen years Jessop led a quiet and uneventful life as the Dominion Immigration Agent. From now on his name rarely appeared in the newspapers. In 1886 the *Colonist* reported a debate in the House of Commons on immigration matters in which E. C. Baker, the Victoria M.P., had "impressed on the Government the desirability and justice of increasing the salary of the immigration agent at Victoria, B.C." He claimed the work entailed on Mr. Jessop was fully as important as that of the agents at Emerson or Brandon and the officers there received $1,400 each. Mr. Carling acknowledged the efficient manner in which Mr. Jessop fulfilled his service and said if there was anything like a large influx of immigrants into Victoria the Government would consider the desirability of increasing his salary.[10]

A few years later the Province of British Columbia re-established its own immigration agency and Jessop returned to his original post as Provincial Immigration Agent under the "Department of Immigration and Education.[11]

In 1897 Jessop lost his wife Margaret, his companion of thirty years, when she suffered a fatal heart attack. Her funeral service, an Anglican one, took place in Victoria's Christ Church Cathedral. She was buried in the new Ross Bay cemetery. In reporting her death the *Colonist* commented that, "Mrs. Jessop has been for upwards of 35 years an honored and respected resident of this city, and to her careful, painstaking instruction many of the present generation of Victorians are indebted for their early initiation into the intricacies of a complete education."[12] Theirs had been a childless marriage, but both loving children, they had adopted a daughter, Jessie Scott. Margaret Jessop, in her will, left her Roseville property of Yates Street to her husband and lots in the James Bay area to her adopted daughter.

John Jessop's official life in later years seemed to offer him little scope for creativity or for the satisfaction of his interests. He had, however, from the year of his first arrival in the colony been closely associated with, and vitally interested in, the work of the Methodist Church. He had helped establish the first Methodist Church in

Victoria (the old Pandora Street Church on land granted by Governor Douglas) and was from the beginning a member of its board. He was secretary of the joint boards of his church until his death.[13]

D. W. Higgins, for long the publisher of the *Colonist,* relates in his book, *The Passing of a Race,* an anecdote involving Jessop in this connection. Victoria in the 1860's had an interesting roustabout-town by the name of John Butt, a petty thief and general vagabond. Butt had been Victoria's first town crier. Equipped with a stentorian voice and ringing a bell, he would stand on the street corners and proclaim sales, theatrical performances or special events. He was fond of singing and this may have accounted for his presence one stormy night at the Methodist Church when Jessop was conducting the meeting. The speaker asked for a glass of water. There being no taps in the church in those days, John Butt jumped up and offered to run out and bring some water. He dashed into the nearest saloon, seized the water jug and said that it was needed at the church. Only a fire could explain Butt wanting water so the occupants of the saloon chased after him to the church and burst into Jessop's meeting with the laudable intention of putting out a fire. When they saw Butt deliver the jug to the speaker, they roared with laughter.[14]

Jessop had been active in establishing the first Methodist Sunday School in Victoria and was its superintendent from 1861 to 1867 when David Spencer, the pioneer merchant, took over this duty. Jessop's interest in music made him an enthusiastic member of his church's choir and for years its choir leader.

In 1869 he was one of four laymen who were given honorary appointments as "exhorters" or lay preachers. He gave continually of his time to church affairs and whenever his church was in financial need he was most generous in his personal contributions to its funds. He was active in the building of both the old Pandora Street Church and the present Metropolitan Church and was a trustee of the property for nearly forty years. In 1891 his name appeared as a trustee and plaintiff for his church in a court action against Amor de Cosmos who had purchased the old Pandora Street church when the congregation moved to the new building.[15] When the first provincial conference of the Methodist Church was held, Jessop was prominent among the leaders and later attended annual conferences of the British Columbia church on several occasions and in 1894 at the General Conference held in Montreal he was an official representative from his province.

In 1898 the *Colonist* carried this brief social note:[16]

MR. JESSOP'S JUBILEE — The fiftieth year of Mr. John Jessop's connection with the Methodist Church was celebrated at the Metropolitan Methodist Church on Friday evening. The school-room of the church was beautifully decorated and the gathering included, besides the pastor and officers of the church, the members of the Ladies' Aid of the church and others. An address was presented to Mr. Jessop by Mr. A. Lee and Mr. M. Baker, while on behalf of the Ladies' Aid Mrs. L. Goodacre presented Mr. Jessop with a purse. Short speeches were made by Sheriff McKillan, Postmaster Shakespeare, Rev. J. C. Speer, Ald. Humber and Rev. Thomas Champness, and Mr. Jessop replied feelingly to the kindly sentiments expressed.

Jessop lived to see the nineteenth century ushered out and the new century in. Since he had landed in Victoria that New Year's Day in 1860 he had watched his adopted home grow from a little colonial village to a modern city of twenty thousand. He had witnessed the shanty town become a city of solid, respectable Victorian brick buildings, the dusty streets paved, and the flickering gas lights give way in the 1880's to electric street lighting. The railways had come in the 1880's, first the Canadian Pacific inching its way to the new upstart port of Vancouver, and then the Esquimalt and Nanaimo Railway which would link Victoria with the "up-Island" towns. By the 1890's the streets which once echoed to the clip-clop of horses' hooves rang with the bells and rattles of electric tramcars and the occasional chugs and splutters of the first automobiles.

He watched, as the years slipped by, the construction of Esquimalt's graving dock and more recently of Victoria's outer harbor wharves. He had seen the shipping in the harbor change from sleek sailing ships, Indian canoes, ornate paddle-wheelers and the grimy sealing fleet to large, modern coal-burning steamships.

About town he had witnessed the erection of new landmarks — the Royal Jubilee Hospital, the City Hall, the large public market building and the ornate Driard Hotel[17] with its red plush splendor and its famous cuisine.

On the James Bay side of the harbor the old colonial parliament buildings, the "Birdcages", had come down and in their place had arisen the glittering be-domed spectacle of the new parliament build-ings, whose architect, enamored of the palaces of Indian princes and Renaissance rulers, had conceived this unique blending of East and West — so suitable for a city with its back to the western world and its face toward Asia.

Of the men who had once decided the destinies of British Columbia in the old colonial buildings, Jessop had seen most pass away — Leonard McClure in 1867, Sir James Douglas in 1877, Rocke Robertson in 1881, Andrew Charles Elliott in 1889, Judge Begbie in 1894 and Amor de Cosmos in 1897.

In his daily walks from his home on Yates Street Jessop now strolled through suburbs with substantial Victorian homes embowered in their lovely gardens and on into the sylvan tranquillity of Beacon Hill Park with its great garry oaks, the green cricket pitch, the little lake alive with water fowl and the clumps of yellow broom. Here he could rest and gaze across the shimmering blue waters of the strait to the snow-capped Olympics beyond.

As he sat there at the turn of the century he may have reflected on the developments which had taken place in this vast province which he had once been privileged to pioneer. The new world port of Vancouver which he had first visited as the sawmill settlement of Granville or "Gastown" had now outstripped in population the capital city. Beyond it and the coastal mountains lay the sunlit valleys of the Interior where new cities had grown up and had been incorporated — Kamloops, Vernon, Penticton, Kelowna, Kaslo and Rossland. A smelter at Trail had commenced operations in 1896. Up the coast sawmills and fish canneries were bringing new wealth from forest and sea. The orchards of the Okanagan Valley were already shipping their fruits to market and the rolling range lands of the Dry Belt were now speckled with herds of white-faced Herefords.

Throughout this fast-growing province, in its cities, towns and hamlets, its children were attending schools which were free to all and free from secretarian differences, and learning, in the fashion of the system which he had established, to become citizens of this land.

On March 30, 1901 the end came to John Jessop as he was hurrying from his office up Government Street. Struck with a heart attack, he collapsed in the street and died.[18]

When he was laid to rest beside his wife in Ross Bay cemetery the Reverend Elliott Rowe expressed the high regard of his friends and the appreciation of the community for the work of John Jessop:

> The most important factor in the strength of a nation is the moral and intellectual quality of its people, especially perhaps of those who lay its earliest foundation . . . To say that John Jessop was a pioneer worker whose efforts were unselfish in motive, exalted in aim and beneficial in results is to state but the simple

truth and to pay a well deserved tribute to his memory. He loyally served his generation . . . The excellence of our present school system is in part the product of the wisdom with which he wrought on its foundations during his occupancy of the office of Superintendent of Education.[19]

In his will Jessop made provision for $3000 to be used for a peal of bells, to be placed in the tower of the Metropolitan Church. When his estate was finally settled (not until 1937) the bells were installed and dedicated as the "John Jessop Memorial Chimes". Each Sunday as they ring out across the city he loved, the voice of John Jessop symbolically speaks again.

Perhaps Hilaire Belloc's lines from *Duncton Hill* are not inappropriate to the memory of this man:

"He does not die who can bequeath
Some influence to the land he knows."

FOOTNOTES

[1] Johnson, F. H., *A History of Public Education in British Columbia,* Publications Centre, University of British Columbia, 1964, pp. 89, 90. The Superintendent and his Deputy had inspected schools in addition to their other duties.

[2] Public Archives of Canada, Sir John A. Macdonald Papers, M. G. 26 A_1 (C) Vol. 305. Senators Richard Wm. Carrall of Barkerville, Wm. John Macdonald of Victoria and Clement Francis Cornwall (later in 1881, Lieut. Governor of British Columbia) from Ashcroft. Edgar Dewdney (Yale), J. S. Thompson (Cariboo) and T. R. McInnes (New Westminster).

[3] C. C. Mackenzie to Jessop, B.C. Superintendent, Ed. Dept., Correspondence Outward, 1879-1882, 10 Nov. 1879, B.C. Archives.

[4] *Canadian Album: Men of Canada,* Brantford, Bradley and Garritson & Co., 1895, vol. IV, p. 87.

[5] *Colonist,* March 30, 1883, p. 2.

[6] Grant, George M., *Ocean to Ocean. Sandford Fleming's Expedition Through Canada in 1872.* Toronto, Belford, 1877, pp. 331, 332.

[7] Jessop to Grant, Grant Papers M.G. 30 D 8, Vol. 5, Oct. 23, 1883, Public Archives of Canada.

[8] Immigration Report, Sessional Papers of British Columbia, 1883-4, p. 297ff.

[9] Sessional Papers of British Columbia, 1884-85, pp. 303-308.

[10] *Colonist,* June 2, 1886, p. 2.

[11] *Colonist,* Oct. 17, 1897, p. 5. Jessop is referred to here as "provincial immigration agent".

[12] *Colonist,* Oct. 17, 1897, pp. 5 and 8, and Oct. 19, p. 5.

[13] Metropolitan United Church, Victoria, 1859-1959. (Centenary Pamphlet).

[14] Higgins, D. W., *The Passing of a Race,* Toronto, Wm. Briggs, 1905, p. 115ff and the *Methodist Recorder,* Victoria, Feb. 1900, p. 9, and April 1901, p. 9. I am also indebted to Mrs. Thelma R. Johns, the historian of the church for much of this information.

[15] *Colonist,* May 23, 1891, p. 3.

[16] *Colonist,* Nov. 20, 1898, p. 3.

[17] This building, at the corner of View and Broad Streets, now forms part of the Eaton's Department store complex.

[18] *Colonist,* March 31, 1901.

[19] "Death of Mr. John Jessop", *Methodist Recorder,* Victoria, April 1901, p. 9.

Bibliography

NEWSPAPERS

British Columbian (New Westminster)
Cariboo Sentinel (Barkerville) 1874-75
Colonist (Victoria). This paper also went at various times under the name of the *British Colonist* and the *Victoria Daily Colonist*.
Nor-Wester (Fort Garry) 1859
Press (Victoria) 1861
Standard (Victoria)
Times (New Westminster) 1859-60
Weekly British Colonist (Victoria)

OFFICIAL PUBLICATIONS

Dawson, S. J. and Hind, Henry Y., *Papers Relative to the Exploration of the Country Between Lake Superior and the Red River Settlement*, London, Queen's Printer, 1859.
Hind, Henry Youle, *Reports of Progress Together with a Preliminary General Report on the Assiniboine and Saskatchewan Exploring Expedition Made Under Instructions from the Provincial Secretary, Canada*, Toronto, Lovell, 1859.
Journal of Education of Upper Canada, Dept. of Education of Upper Canada.
Journals and Sessional Papers of British Columbia from 1872 to 1879. These contain the Annual Reports of the Superintendent of Education including statistical tables and appendixes.
Province of British Columbia, Information for Intending Settlers. Published by the Government of Canada, Dept. of Agriculture, 1886.
Province of British Columbia. Journals of the Legislative Assembly.
Sessional Papers of British Columbia, 1883 to 1885, Immigration Reports.

UNPUBLISHED MANUSCRIPTS

Annual Reports of the Local Superintendent of Common Schools for the Townships of Whitby, Whitby East and Southwold, 1855 to 1858, Ontario Archives.
Board of Education of Vancouver Island, Minutes of the Board, 1872-78, B.C. Archives.
Colonial Office, Blue Book of Statistics on Schools in British Columbia from 1865 to 1870. National Archives, Ottawa, CO 64/6 to 64/11.
Correspondence Outward of the Superintendent of Education, 1872 to 1882, B.C. Archives.

Diary of R. M. Clemitson, School Inspector, 1876-77, B.C. Archives.

Jessop, John, Inspectoral Diary 1872-1874, B.C. Archives.

Jessop, John, Miscellaneous Papers, B.C. Archives.

Macdonald, Margaret Lillooet, "New Westminster 1859-1871", M.A. History Thesis, University of British Columbia, 1947.

Reid, James Gordon, "John Robson and the British Columbian", M.A. Thesis, University of British Columbia, 1950.

Register of School Teachers, 1872-79, B.C. Provincial Secretary, Board of Education, B.C. Archives.

Training Register of the Toronto Normal School, 1852-55, Ontario Archives.

Waddington, Alfred, Journal of Alfred Waddington, Superintendent of Education for Vancouver Island, School Visits, 1865-67, B.C. Archives.

Walden, Frederick E., "The Social History of Victoria, B.C., 1858-1871", B.A. Honours Essay, University of British Columbia, 1951.

BOOKS

Adams, Emma H., *To and Fro, Up and Down,* Cincinnati, Cranston, 1888.

Balf, Mary, Kamloops. *A History of the District up to 1914,* Kamloops Museum, 1969.

The Canadian Album. Men of Canada, Brantford, Bradley, Garritson and Co., 1895, vol. 4, p. 87.

Downs, Art, *Wagon Road North. The Story of the Cariboo Gold Rush in Historical Photos,* Quesnel, Northwest Digest Ltd., 1960.

Dufferin, Lady, *My Canadian Journal,* (Edited by Gladys C. Walker), Don Mills, Longmans, 1969.

Elliott, Gordon R., *Quesnel, Commercial Centre of the Cariboo Gold Rush,* Quesnel, Cariboo Observer, 1958.

Fawcett, Edgar, *Some Reminiscences of Old Victoria,* Toronto, Wm. Briggs, 1912.

Gosnell, R. E., *The Year Book of British Columbia, Victoria, 1911.*

Guillet, E. C., *The Story of Canadian Roads,* University of Toronto Press, 1964.

Grant, George M., *Ocean to Ocean. Sandford Fleming's Expedition Through Canada in 1872,* Toronto, Belford Bros., 1877.

Hargrave, Joseph James, *Red River,* Montreal, Lovell, 1871.

Higgins, D. W., *The Passing of the Race,* Toronto, Wm. Briggs, 1905.

Jackman, S. W., *Portraits of the Premiers,* Sidney, Gray's Publishing Co., 1969.

Johnson, F. Henry, *A Brief History of Canadian Education,* Toronto, McGraw-Hill, 1968.

— *A History of Public Education in British Columbia,* Vancouver, University of British Columbia Publications Centre, 1964.

Johnson, R. Byron, *Very Far West Indeed,* London, Sampson Low, 1872.

Kerr, J. B., *Biographical Dictionary of Well-Known British Columbians,* Vancouver, Kerr and Begg, 1895.

Leggo, Wm., *The History of the Administration of the Right Honourable Frederick Temple, Earl of Dufferin,* Montreal, Lovell and Toronto, Mercer Adam, 1878.

Lowther, Barbara J., *A Bibliography of British Columbia. Laying the Foundations, 1849-1899,* University of Victoria, 1968.

MacFie, Matthew, *Vancouver Island and British Columbia. Their History, Resources and Prospects,* London, Longman Green, 1865.

McKelvie, B. C., *Pageant of British Columbia,* Toronto, Thos. Nelson and Sons, 1957.

172

Mather, Barry and McDonald, Margaret, *New Westminster, the Royal City,* Toronto, J. M. Dent, 1958.

Metropolitan United Church 1859-1959, Victoria, 1959.

Molyneux, St. John, *The Sea of Mountains, An Account of Lord Dufferin's Tour Through British Columbia in 1876,* London, Hurst and Blackett, 1877, vols. 1 and 2.

Morton, A. S., *A History of the Canadian West to 1870-71,* Toronto, Thos. Nelson and Sons.

Nesbitt, James K., *Album of Victoria Old Homes and Families,* Victoria, Hebden, 1956.

Ormsby, Margaret A., *British Columbia: A History,* Toronto, MacMillans, 1958.

Pemberton, J. Despard, *Facts and Figures Relating to Vancouver Island and British Columbia,* London, Longman Green, 1860.

Pethick, Derek, *James Douglas: Servant of Two Empires,* Vancouver, Mitchell Press, 1969.

Pethick, Derek, *Victoria, the Fort,* Vancouver, Mitchell Press, 1968.

Phillips, C. E., *The Development of Education in Canada,* Toronto, W. J. Gage, 1957.

Reid, J. H. Stewart, *Mountains, Men and Rivers. British Columbia in Legend and Story,* Toronto, Ryerson, 1954.

Shelton, W. George, *British Columbia and Confederation,* University of Victoria Press, 1967.

Southesk, Earl of, *Saskatchewan and the Rocky Mountains. A Diary and Narrative of Travel, Sport, and Adventure, During a Journey Through the Hudson's Bay Company's Territories in 1859 and 1860,* Edmonton, M. G. Hurtig, 1969.

Spry, Irene M., *The Palliser Expedition: An Account of John Palliser's British North American Expedition 1857-1860,* Toronto, MacMillan, 1963.

Victoria, Historical Review 1862-1962, Centennial Society, 1962.

Victoria Illustrated, Victoria, B.C., 1891.

Wild, Roland, *Amor De Cosmos,* Toronto, Ryerson Press, 1958.

ARTICLES

Balf, Mary, "Cache Creek School was Interior's First". *Kamloops Daily Sentinel,* Apr. 27, 1968, p. 3.

— "Settlers' Children Trekked Long Distance to School", *Kamloops Daily Sentinel,* May 11, 1968, p. 3.

Campbell, Burt R., "From Hand-set to Linotype", *B.C. Historical Quarterly,* vol. 10, no. 4, Oct. 1946, pp. 253 to 272.

Cowan, Anna M., "Memories of Upper Fort Garry", *The Beaver,* vol. 266, no. 2, Sept. 1935, pp. 25-30.

"Death of Mr. John Jessop", *Methodist Recorder,* Victoria, Apr. 1901, p. 9.

Gosnell, R. E., "History of Education in British Columbia" in Hopkins, J. Castell, *Canada, An Encyclopedia of the Country,* Toronto, Linscott, 1898, vol. III, pp. 240-245.

Hacking, Norman R., "B.C. Steamboat Days 1870-1883", *B.C. Historical, Quarterly,* vol. II, no. 2, Apr. 1947, pp. 69-112.

Higgins, Stella, "British Columbia and the Confederation Era" in *British Columbia and Confederation,* University of Victoria, 1967, p. 27.

Ireland, Willard E. (ed.), "Gold Rush Days in Victoria 1858-1859", *B.C. Historical Quarterly,* vol. 12, no. 3, July 1948, pp. 231-246.

Jessop, John, "Over the Plains in '59", Victoria, *Colonist,* a series of articles beginning with the issue of Jan. 1, 1890, p. 3.

"Leading Laymen. Mr. John Jessop", *Methodist Recorder,* Victoria, Feb. 1900, p. 9.

McKelvie, B.C., "Lt. Col. Israel Wood Powell, M.D., C.M.", *B.C. Historical Quarterly,* vol. II, no. 1, Jan. 1947, pp. 33-54.

Nesbitt, James K., "He Fought for Schools", *Victoria Daily Colonist,* July 29, 1956, p. 5.

Palliser, John, "Progress of the British North American Exploring Expedition Under the Command of Capt. John Palliser, F.R.G.S.", *Proceedings of the Royal Geographical Society,* 1880, pp. 267 to 314.

Robinson, A., "History of Education in British Columbia", in Shortt, A. and Doughty, A. G. (ed.), *Canada and Its Provinces,* vol. 22, pp. 401 to 442.

Sage, Walter N., "Federal Parties and Provincial Groups", *B.C. Historical Quarterly,* vol. 12, no. 2, Apr. 1948, pp. 151-169.

— "From Colony to Province", *B.C. Historical Quarterly,* Vol. 3, no. 1, Jan. 1939, pp. 1-14.

Smith, Dorothy Blakey (ed.), "Harry Guillod's Journal of a Trip to Cariboo, 1862", *B.C. Historical Quarterly,* vol. 19, nos. 3 and 4, July and October 1955, pp. 187-232.

Spragge, George W., "An Early Letter from Victoria, V. I.", *Canadian Historical Review,* University of Toronto Press, vol. 29, 1948, pp. 54-56.

"Two Narratives of the Fraser River Gold-Rush", *B.C. Historical Quarterly,* vol. 5, no. 3, Victoria, July 1941, pp. 221-232.

Waites, J. A., "Responsible Government and Confederation: The Popular Movement for Popular Government", *B.C. Historical Quarterly,* vol. 6, no. 2, Apr. 1942, pp. 119ff.

Willis, J. West, "Staging in the Cariboo", *B.C. Historical Quarterly,* vol. 12, no. 3, July 1948, pp. 185-209.

Wolfenden, Madge, "Early Government Gazettes", *B.C. Historical Quarterly,* vol. 7, no. 3, July 1943, pp. 171-190.

Index

JESSOP'S ROUTES
FROM CANADA ··········
TO THE GOLDFIELDS ----
ELECTIONEERING IN THE
KOOTENAYS ·-·-·-·